Nightmares Echo

Katlyn Stewart

PublishAmerica
Baltimore

First printing

ISBN: 1-59286-622-0
PUBLISHED BY PUBLISHAMERICA BOOK PUBLISHERS
www.publishamerica.com
Baltimore

Printed in the United States of America

Dedications:

To my Husband - who had the most profound impact on my life, the one that tore down the walls I had built around me, stood by me, and truly loved me...allowing me to shine through with strength and determination.

To my children and grandchildren... through their eyes I was able to see what being a child of innocence and wonder is all about.

To my family and friends who stood by me no matter what.

And to Mom..

CHAPTER ONE

And so this story begins...

Let me take you, the reader back to the beginning... the beginning of all that made me, me. When I was two years old I was diagnosed as having been born without a bladder muscle. From the age of two and until the age of fourteen I had eight major operations, and over twelve minor operations, to either shape a new bladder or to reinstall a much larger one to go with my growing stages in life.

My early memories are filled with Doctor visits and hospitalizations. I had become such a champ, that by the time I was seven years old that I no longer was afraid to stay by myself at night in the hospital without my Mommy.

As you can probably imagine, I had a scar down near what we would later call my "bikini area"; though instead of being parallel with my hip bones it ran up and down, and it was **not** your usual thin-lined scar I might add either, for it seems that the Doctors at the time thought it necessary to utilize the same site each time I needed surgery. By the time I was nine years old and fully capable of most memories, I already felt disfigured and certainly different than my other female family members.

It is also safe to assume that by this time my self confidence was not growing by leaps and bounds. Due to the fact that I knew my body looked different without clothing I was very cautious about anyone, even my own mother seeing me naked, because in my mind I was "ugly" down there in my private places. I knew I didn't look like my mother.. nor did I look like my sister. Every teen magazine I looked at had cute little girls in sweet-looking bikini's: something that I could never dare to wear for fear that my scar would show above the line.

There were other things taking place within me: I had started to develop breasts, and I had started my period, something that mothers and daughters did not discuss, so that I was not really sure what these changes that were taking place meant. Oh, what a year to begin remembering....

CHAPTER TWO

The first recollection that I have of any sexual abuse was when I was nine years old, but prior to that I have no real memories of any other events, so for my own piece of mind... nine was when it started.

At first I guess it was innocent enough, after all as a child you tend to look at your "Daddy" as some sort of hero. So an extra hug, that extra kiss on the mouth, any extra attention doesn't send any bells or whistles going off. You just think to yourself how special you are that Daddy spends so much attention on you. What a lucky little girl you must be. An extra special dress, an extra special Barbie doll, and extra special hugs and kisses. I especially thought that I was getting all of this wonderful attention to having to be in and out of Doctors office and hospitals so much, and I guess the other family members must have thought the same as well.

My Mother had just become ill during the start of this period in my life. She was a wonderfully sweet woman, and appeared so beautiful to me with her auburn hair and bright green eyes, so full of love and laughter, who while at work one afternoon fell from a chair that broke beneath her, crashing her down on the concrete floor. She destroyed several discs in her back, and would have to under go several back surgeries and spinal fusion's to repair the damage and ease the pain throughout the next few years. She was put on a lot of medications to help her deal with her pain. There were many times I had to see my

Mother lying in the bed with her legs being held up by a contraption, so that she could not roll over. She would just have to lay on her back, and only get up long enough to go to the bathroom.

Unfortunately, she was never the same after all that she had been through, and had permanent back stiffness and pain and was finally disabled from work .

It was also during these times while Mom was in the hospital, there was extra chores put upon me. My brother and sister were a little young yet to handle a lot of the responsibilities : there was dinner to cook so that Dad could come home, eat, and go to visit Mom in the hospital. There was laundry to wash so that we had clean clothes for school, and dishes and vacuuming to do, none of which I minded doing as it made me feel like such a "big" girl.. A young "mommy", that years later I would realized maybe I was a "young mommy" in too many ways.

I can not honestly tell you when the innocent feelings went away and the scared and confused feelings started setting in, but somewhere in my tenth year, I knew something was not right. Dad was becoming too nice, there where too many touches that didn't feel like nice touches. Too many times having him touch me in places that my mom had told me that no one was to touch unless you're washing yourself. I had one too many bouts with fevers where he had to check my temperature under my blouse...

It was during this time that I was a becoming a portly little thing, and food was becoming a dear friend of mine. I loved to eat...though more times than not I am sure it wasn't out of hunger. I look back at it all now and I have come to realize that I ate to become heavy, and even in my young mind I wanted to look bad - that if I looked bad, perhaps my Father would leave me alone. Deep down even as young as I was, I knew what was happening in my life did not feel right by any respect.

I started writing poetry, it helped to jot down on paper the feelings I had. The poetry was dark and foreboding...but it was my only outlet.

I started clinging to my Mother more and more, and going to my Grandma's house as often as she and my Papa would let me, every weekend and every summer, if I could. It was also the time that I found my first "best" friend, Kelly Jenkins.

Kelly lived down the street from me and though she was two years younger, was probably a lot more mature than I was. If I wasn't begging to go to Grandma and Papa's house, then I was begging to go to Kelly's till my Mom would give in and let me go. It was at Grandma's that I could just be a little girl. I could play with my dolls, sing songs with my Grandma, eat fresh Peaches with my Papa, play with my cousins, and have no fear of anyone or anything hurting me. My Papa would protect me and make me feel secure. I could get a hug from him, and didn't have to be afraid of what he might do... Kelly's house would offer me happiness and laughter with someone around my age, we could play dress up, play our records, talk about boys and laugh.

By escaping to someone else's house I could forget what was happening at home. I was becoming too much of an adult in my own home. I could just be me and enjoy being a kid when I was outside of it...and being away from home meant being away from the unpleasant things that were my daily life. No one knew the deep and dirty secrets that lay inside of my house, so when I was outside of its four walls... I could pretend like they didn't exist, and that the things happening to me didn't really exist....

CHAPTER THREE

By the time I had turned thirteen I had withdrawn within myself. The child that used to laugh and tell stupid jokes to get my Mother to laugh was now gone. I was becoming shy, and felt homely-looking and fat...ugly. My Father was not helping matters much either. He would tell me how ugly I was becoming, how homely I was starting to look, how misshapen my body had become. He told me that no boy would want someone like me, and that I should be grateful that "Daddy" cared so much. I believed every word, and every look in the mirror was a reflection of what he said I was. I found nothing about me appealing. My Aunt, my Father's sister, wasn't helping either...Aunt Margaret would put me on diet after diet to lose the weight. She babysat my brother, sister, and I on occasion. While the other children would enjoy a full meal of whatever she had fixed, I would get a salad and a hard boiled egg. She would tell me how ridiculous I looked in some of the clothing I wore to cover up my figure. She would make me feel uglier than I already felt that I was.

My Father had upgraded his touching now to include masturbation of himself while I lay there in my bed. He would come into the room and remove his boxer shorts. I would cover up my face and body as well as I could with my covers to hide myself from it...but still could here the "swishing" sound being made. It was an eerie sound to me, it made me sick to my stomach to hear it, and I was always grateful when he was done

10

and I could finally go to sleep.

Even though my life was anything but normal, I was still a girl of thirteen, with thoughts and feelings of my own starting to emerge, no matter what my Father had said about me and my body, or how worthless I was. I still had begun to notice boys, and had even had a few "boy-friends" even though we never actually went anywhere or did anything. Except for one boy I had met in school, Josh.

I had a huge crush on this already six foot boy that was so much older than me - 15. He was in my class at school and I thought he was so handsome. Mom had let me and a couple of friends go to the fair. She would stay outside the midway and look at the exhibits, and wait for me to go out and ride some of the rides with my friends. It offered me a little freedom, and I was so excited about feeling independent of my parents. Though it was not planned, Josh was there at the fair too. He asked me to walk around the Fairgrounds with him and he took me on the ride called "the Himalayan"...a fast ride that went both forward and backwards at rapid speed with loud music playing and strobe lights flashing. It was while on that ride, and while "Mother and Child Reunion" played, that I got my first French kiss...a memory I still hold to this day because of the power and feelings that stirred from that one little kiss. Josh and I did not remain boyfriend and girlfriend for very long, but the power of that kiss and the excitement that surrounded it made me feel alive for the first time.

I was by now keeping my secret of sexual abuse well hidden from my girlfriends, and my occasional hand-holding/smooching boyfriends. With each boyfriend I had, Father became more tightly controlling about me, and deciding that I was too young to venture out and do things with the other teens my age.

His anger would flare and he would end up embarrassing me when a boy showed up at the door un-announced. A lot of arguments started raging in my household because my Mother wanted me to go and have fun while Father wanted me to stay home and away from the "boys".

I realize now that this was his form of jealousy, and that his anger over a boy coming to visit only fueled it. I guess in his mind, I was his to manipulate and threaten, and that by my venturing out to be around boys, he would somehow lose his stranglehold on me.

Dad was now threatening me more than ever in order to keep up his "game playing". The threats would consist of "if I ever told Mom he would do one of two things: have her sent away.. or have me sent to a home for wayward girls", because he would guarantee that no one would ever believe me over him.

I believed those threats too; Mom had been very ill by this time and on a lot of medications - I really believed that he would have her or me put away. After all, he was well known in his community and church as an upstanding pillar, with a well recognized long standing name. Who on this earth would have believed me, a young girl over anything he would have to say?

He was still touching me and masturbating himself. I would just lay in my bed, on my stomach, stiff as a board and cry softly to myself and plead with God to make him stop and go away. I would beg God to make my Mom walk into the room, because if she saw it with her own two eyes...then he could not do anything to anyone, I would finally have someone's belief in me... but, it didn't stop... and mom didn't come in...and my sister did not wake up to find him there and rescue me...and God never sent a bolt of lightning to hit him...and it all continued night after night.

I tried everything to get through the nights. I would beg him over and over not to do this.. but he would continue. I would cry.. but he would continue...I would fight his hands off of me but time kept spinning along. I would go to bed at night and wrap myself tightly in my blanket, laying face down with only the back of my head being exposed. I wore full top and bottom pajama's...I tried to think of any and everything I could to stop him. I even tried to threaten him, which only caused me more problems.

He stepped up his plans to have me sent away, and even got information from a clinic on the mental hospital in an adjoining town. His threats had also turned into a new and different directions: I was not to have new clothes, unless I did what he asked. There would be nothing new bought for me, no matter if it was a necessity or not. I could not get my hair trimmed or paint my nails... things that were important to a young girl. When my Mom would ask why I couldn't have something, he would make up a lie about something I did or didn't do, and tell her that I was grounded until further notice until I straightened up. My Mom would believe him and he would get his way.

And if I had truly gone against him the night before, than he would make a point to embarrass me in front of my friends, and even my family members. I remember vividly the times we went to visit my Grandma's house, how I treasured going to see her, only to have my Father say things about me, making me sound like a bad child...lying or whatever he needed to do to convince them that I never did right, never listened.

I would then have to look in my Grandma's eyes and see that she was not happy with me, and there was nothing I could say to her, I could not tell her the truth. It would break her heart.

So.. I stopped my threats.. and started resigning myself to the fact that I had to deal with this.. to live with this.

Then one night the White Knight came; well in my dreams that is. I guess my mind I started playing make-believe to get through the nights and actually got so good that I could tone out everything that was going on around me. All I had to do was call out for my White Knight to rescue me.. and he would come into my room, on his beautiful black horse and grab my hand and free me from my Father and lift me onto the horse and ride away with me into the night.

I never saw his face, but he was strong and could defeat my Father and take me away. I would hold tightly to him; he would not utter a word... but I was safe...and free...and felt no sadness.. no pain.

For a little time in my life now, my life became a little easier to deal with. It was getting easier to escape reality and get away from the horrible feeling that I felt deep in the pit of my stomach....

It was getting easier to sleep at night after my Father left the room. I was learning to disassociate myself from what I was unable to deal with in my life.

CHAPTER FOUR

I wish I could say that the White Knight kept rescuing me each and every night, but unfortunately the older I got, the more things my father decided to try with me. He was, I guess, getting bored with the whole touch- me- masturbate- himself technique that he had been doing as of late. He wanted me to become an active participant, to touch him with my hands.

It was getting harder to focus in on my White Knight.. when your constantly fighting someone's hands touching you, fighting away from a hand that wants you to touch him. I could not give in to it, could not make myself do it... and of course I would pay for it during the day. Even as young as I was, knowing the trouble I would be in; I still had a bit of fight and courage deep within me, yet I stayed frightened of him.

I would lay so still in the softly lit room and make myself try harder to bring in the Knight. Sometimes it worked so easily and at other times.. it was a major chore. Father's hands would reach in between my legs and I would fight them off of me with all the strength I could find. The anger he had toward me for not giving in to him intensified.. There were times I wished I was dead, and at other times, I prayed for him to die.

Every movement I made, was now watched. If I spent the night at a friends house, he would drive up and down the street in front of the friends house all during the night I was there. It was getting harder and harder to make up excuses for why he would do this - and to all the friends I had, I must have been the most untrusted child in America.

But I would make up excuse after excuse as to why my father did what he did. My telephone conversations were monitored, my school books gone through at random, looking for anything he could use against me. The least little thing he thought I might have done wrong, brought on more whippings with a belt. Still I would try to stay strong and hold firm. But, in the end my father would basically win out; no matter how strong I tried to stay.

His driving up and down the road my friends lived on while I was there, unnerved them, and eventually I would stop being asked to spend the night by all of my friends but one...Kelly. She didn't ask why anymore and I didn't tell. We were as close as two friends could be except for the secrets that I had and couldn't share. In my mind I believed somehow that I had brought this on, had deserved the torment in my life. Part of me even believed that this was the way it was supposed to be.. that all little girls must do this for their Fathers. So, why would I burden Kelly with what was going on in my life.....

But...thanks to my Father...the secrets did come out...I had invited Kelly to spend the night with me. We were having a great time listening to music in my room, Father was being nice and leaving us alone to ourselves and we had went to bed at a decent time by my Father's standards. But during the wee hours of the night, Kelly woke me up and told me she wanted to go home, she was in tears and said that she was sick to her stomach.

She wanted my Mom and not my Dad to take her home, and Mom did.. Kelly only lived down the block so it was not a huge problem...and I genuinely thought that she was sick and had wanted her mother. However, I found out the next day when visiting her that she had not been sick...but had been sickened by my Father... touching her.

The cat was out of the bag so to speak. She had not told her Mother yet because my Father had whispered to her the same type of threats he had done to me the countless times before. I broke down in tears in her bedroom and all the dirty, nasty, laundry that I had kept hidden came spilling out.

She didn't judge.. she didn't run and get her Mom.. she just sat there and listened to everything I said... and tried to be as reassuring as she could, without really even knowing how. She promised me that she would never tell my story, and by doing that, she promised to never tell anyone what had happened to her. I was just 14 and she, just 12.

I look back now and reflect on that afternoon in her room and the secret I shared with her and the bond of secrecy I asked her to commit to....and then...I look at my own 12- year-old daughter and wonder to myself : how were we ever strong enough to deal with these things at such an early age?

I also now had a confidant, I could tell Kelly everything I was living with...I no longer had to live with it bottled up inside all of the time, I had a way to release the anger and pain that had been stored up so long.

I was getting old enough to baby sit the children living in our community, and was so proud of the money I made each week from babysitting in the evening and on week-ends. I bought my first diary which I hid very well in my room, I could write down everything that happened to me during the night and it would help to ease the pain I felt...and dear Kelly never seemed to mind the countless talk sessions we had. I guess she knew that it needed to be gotten out, and she probably felt sorry for me that I had to go through so much turmoil, when the only turmoil she was dealing with at her young age was what boyfriend she wanted, or what new outfit she wanted to save to get next.

My White Knight still came and rescued me late at night sometimes when my mind just couldn't handle it anymore... when I had no more fight left within me and I would finally give in to him. ....I was trying desperately to becoming a little stronger within myself, mostly due to my reliance on the White Knight and Kelly....and like the White Knight, Kelly had become a type of security blanket too.. that I could hold onto when I needed her most.

She was also as I said, more mature in some ways than I was. She had come from a broken home, with a Mother that dated, something rare to see in my day of two- parent families, so her life had been a lot more relaxed and freer than mine. She had already been in more serious relationships, gone much farther with the boys than I had ever dared too...before I had even realized yet what the whole boy-girl thing was all about. I started to feel a little of the shyness fade away. I was getting older and stronger. I was protected during the night by the White Knight living within my mind, and with Kelly there to talk to, I was gaining a little bit of myself...and a little of the spirit that would eventually become me, started to set in.....or so I had thought.

I awoke one morning to screams, sounds like I had never heard before. I ran out of my room to find my younger sister Gale screaming and crying, our mother laying on the floor. In the whirl going on around me and the ambulance coming and leaving... I found that my Mother had overdosed on pills, she was rushed to the hospital and would spend the next week or so in the psychiatric unit there. My Father came home that evening to tell us that Mother had tried to commit suicide, that she didn't just accidentally over dose on her medication. The first thing that came to my head when I learned that was that I had somehow brought it on.

I just knew that she had found out the deep dark secret of what my Father was doing and it was more than she could bear...maybe she had found my diary that I kept with all the dirty secrets deep within it. I didn't know...I just knew it had to have been something that I had done.

While my mother lay in the hospital recuperating from the overdose, my Father stepped up his torment of me...only I had no way out of it this time. He was the law and with my Mother not being there... there was no place for me to go and no one to talk to. I could not get to Kelly's house to get her comfort and understanding, I could not call her on the phone, I did not have her shoulder to cry on.

I would endure the whippings just because "I needed it". It was me.. and the house and the children.. and HIM.

All of the confidence I had started to gain, he was replacing with the self-doubt's again. I was only as confident as a child could be with a friend that listened to her pain and helped her through it.

I was needed to much at home now, to many things needed to be taken care of with the house now that Mom was so ill. I was now closed off from the only releases I had known... he was making very sure of it. He told me over and over that my mother did what she did because I was bad and had not done what he wanted me to do. He made implications that because my Mom had been so sick it had been my duty to take care of his needs. I had not been a good daughter, I had already believed that anyway. So it was easy for him to instill it in me even farther.

I had went against him when he wanted to touch me... I thought I had gotten smart and had stopped him at this new game before it started...I was so wrong. He forced the issue harder...he pushed his threats against me even more.

The daily life became more like a living hell. I had to listen to his threats, deal with arguing back and have to resign myself that whether or not I liked it, he would enter my room at night., night after night.

If I kept fighting...If I refused to give in, then I was going to pay for it...

One night... deep in the middle of my sleep.. I felt something between my legs, I reached down with my hand and felt his head.. I don't believe it takes an expert for anyone to figure out what was going on. I shoved his head away with my hands ...sat up quickly with my back against the wall... and vomited all over myself, the bed and him.

If there had been an ounce of innocence, or a bit of a child left within me, it was now gone. If there had been any self assurance developing it was gone ...the pretty dresses and new toys would all be gone now too. He made it very clear that I would only get the clothes my Brother handed down to me from now on. He hoped I would be ridiculed in school by my appearance and that I would eventually give into the pressures. What he didn't know was I had just enough fight in me that I made a vow I would never give in...I would not allow him to do something like he had tried this time, ever again.

I realized the battle lines were drawn... and the threats and the cruelty would escalate...but I would learn to live with it, somehow. I would will The White Knight to return... I so desperately needed something to hold on to... something to believe in... He was my silent salvation, He saved me, believed in me, he would take me away from the pain. I could go into a peaceful sleep if he came to my side....

My Mother came home from the hospital, and she was unusually quiet and withdrawn, her memories fuzzy. I learned that while she had been in the hospital, they had done Electric Shock Treatments on her...I didn't quite understand what that all meant back then. I just knew that my Mother's once twinkling green eyes looked dark and hollow... and that her personality seemed withdrawn and sad. I don't begin to understand it, and she can't explain what had happened to her or who, for that matter, allowed it to happen.

The stress of everything I am dealing with causes me to go from eating everything I can get my hands on at my whopping 155 lbs on my 4'11" frame, down to 95 lbs in no time. I didn't feel like eating, the look of food making me sick to my stomach... Mother started to worry about me, but I told her I was fine. I move my food around my plate and eat a few bites here and there to make it look like I have eaten, at least something.

CHAPTER FIVE

Kelly's brother, Jack drives up in my driveway on the back of a motorcycle. The driver of this motorcycle, a man I have never seen before...takes off his helmet and sits the helmet on the handle bars. I think he is at least twenty. My heart is pounding out of my chest and I just know that he can see that I can not breath. Every other girl standing there at the moment is giggling and grabbing articles of his for their hope chest, I think they are acting stupid.

I stand firmly planted, I look disinterested., but in actuality I was unable to move for fear of falling down and looking stupid. He ask me questions...I don't have much to say. I remain quiet...mostly because I can not speak. My tongue is much too large at this moment and I believe I might begin to choke.

I appear to be a snob to him...oh, if he only knew. My feelings are nowhere what they appear to be. I am terrified, mystified, and intrigued. I am all of 14 years old and he is the first male figure that has come into my life and made my heart pound like that.

I know what Kelly had been trying to tell me about men and love... and I am thinking by all standards I am instantly in love with an older man.... Jack introduced Chase Michaels to the crowd of girls standing in my yard. I wish I could tell you more about that brief time when the clock stood still, but in all honesty...I can not. I have no idea if I found out his age then or not... but, he was 15.

I can tell you I thought he was older. I can tell you he had crystal blue eyes, a dark tan, and was tall and built husky. I can also tell you that when I walked into the house after meeting him, my mother asked who he was, and my reply was "the man I am going to marry," and that my mother laughed.. and I can still hear that laughter to this very day.

Ahh... but here was a real live version of my fantasized White Knight. He did not have the beautiful horse, but instead a shiny blue motorcycle. He might very well have been the devil himself... it didn't matter to me. He paid attention to me. He winked at me when he spoke, his voice deep and dark. He would speak to me over the crowd of girls...he would search me out when I was walking to the bus stop. He walked with me to the classes at school. He smelled like falling rain.

He asked me to go steady... over all the other girls he could have picked in our school - Me.. homely, ugly, not quite shapely.. me.

Of course, I said "yes" but, I was not allowed to date at 14, although my Mother saw no reason why he couldn't come over and sit on the couch with me and watch television once in a while. My Father would sit there and stare at us as if he could kill one or both of us…and I would pay for being with Chase every night under my Father's hateful eyes. But, nothing my Father said, and none of the ugly words he called me (whore, slut), changed my wanting to be near Chase. It was too wonderful of a feeling to let go of, and my White Knight that had protected me from my nights would now be replaced by Chase Michaels.

Chase was a complex type of guy... and as I said before, he intrigued me. There was several occasions, down at Kelly's house, where Chase could have tried something with me. But he never did. He was too patient, too understanding…as if somehow he knew that I was to fragile yet to be taken beyond the steps of kissing or hugging. Maybe Kelly had told him, maybe he instinctively knew... all of his other friends were "going all the way", and most of my friends were too. Yet he made no attempt to force the issue with me and for that, I was grateful.

I was also venturing out to find more friends my own age, at least trying to. I was not a very outgoing kind of person. Very choosy of people and untrusting, making friends had always been hard for me to do, and most of the friends I had I had gotten because they lived in the community or were friends of Kelly's. Kelly knew me inside out, but we were not the same age nor went to the same school. So I tried relating to other girls my own age…and learn to enjoy what other girls my age would do…share stories of their boyfriends.

CHAPTER SIX

Now Jennifer Samson...she was cool to the bone. She was overweight, and yet it didn't seem to slow her down, with the multitude of friends and boyfriends she had. Jennifer took to me like a sick cat. As quiet as I was, she was just the opposite...fun-loving, carefree, and a true comedian. The friendship would grow into a solid relationship. When I finally thought I could trust her, I spilled all of the dirty secrets to her one evening while spending the night with her. She was so understanding, expressed her emotions to the story I told her, first anger and then tears. But like Kelly, she promised to keep the secrets to herself.

My Father was till the same, he absolutely hated when Mother would let me go to Jennifer's house - after all it was not down the street from us, but across town...so he would have to come up with bigger excuses to leave the house and drive up and down Jennifer's road. Oh he would still do it, but I imagine that it was more difficult to come up with a story that didn't involve the neighborhood 7-11 store (the story he would tell Mother so that he had a reason to leave and go to driving up and down Kelly's road).

It was also during this time that I finally told Chase all the ugly secrets I had been keeping to myself. The minute I told him, he wanted to go and kill my Father, but after I told him the threats against my Mother and myself, he decided he would wait till the right time...He was still young, young in an adults eyes... so if he had done something, anything, no one would have believed him anymore than they would have believed me. One afternoon, and for the life of me I don't know which argument I had gotten into with my Father, or about what…but I made the decision to run away. The molestations were still taking place, not at the level he wanted, and I was starting to recapture some of the self- confidence I needed to become a young adult….but the stress I had been dealing with, the constant nightmares and the weight fluctuations, had somehow all come to a head.

Chase's sister Terri was leaving with her boyfriend to move to Crystal River. Terri told me about the details and when they would be leaving. I begged her to let me go with them. Terri had a young son, Mark, so I asked if I could go and live with them and take care of Mark during the day while they worked. Terri's boyfriend, Patch, (whom I never found out his real name) said I could go. They would meet me at the High School after class. I only told two people, Jennifer and Chase, that I was leaving,.

Chase was going to come and be with me within the year and we would start our lives together there in Crystal River... I would never have to live at home again.

I went to School as normal, only instead of going to class I got in Patch's truck that was parked in the Juniors parking lot. I was so nervous at first, but the further away from home I got, the easier and freer I felt. For four days I would live a life of freedom - I went to bed on those nights with no fear of my Father coming in the room. My days filled with cleaning the house, cooking and watching Mark.

It didn't last long…

On the fifth morning, Patch came in with a worried look to his face. He had been to the gas station down the road and the owner, which he knew, said that the Police had been there looking for him in connection to a missing girl. They had my picture taped to the glass of the station window. My parents had filed Statutory rape charges against him. Patch said that even though he hated to take me home, he had to. He had been in jail a long time ago, and that this charge wasn't something he or I could fight.

I cried…I didn't want to go….not back there. But there was no other choices to make. I couldn't go to my Grandma or my Aunt Elda's house without having to tell them why I didn't want to go back to my own home. I couldn't do that and risk one of them confronting my Father and then him do something terrible to Mother.

So, I packed up my bag of clothes and Patch drove me back to the edge of where I lived, a few streets away, being careful to watch for any police cars.

I walked home and made up a story about being in Naples and living on the streets, and I stuck to the story so that they could not go after Patch or Terri for anything. The police came and took the same statement, seemed satisfied with it, and then had the charges against Patch removed. When they left it allowed my Father and all his anger to shine through.

When he was done with me I was grounded from leaving the house for all but going to school... and I was not allowed to see Chase anymore. My heart was breaking. I knew my life would be a hell like I had never known before. There would be no place to go to laugh, no way to get the stress of this house off of my shoulders. I would once again be under my Father's watchful eyes all the time and would have to deal with him coming into my room again.

My Father screamed at me for what seemed like an eternity, my Mother just sitting there not uttering a word. He finally sent me to my room, and I ran there crying. My emotions were at their peak. My Mother came into the room right after that and sat down next to me on the bed. I thought she was going to yell at me also, I thought she would be so angry at me for running away from home like some juvenile brat. Instead I was shocked at what she did do.

She reached over and touched my leg as I sat there crying, and the words she spoke I will never forget :"**I know.. I know.. I read your diary**". Her words were soft, as she whispered this to me. I cried even harder. Oh God… I was so ashamed that my Mother had read all of the terrible things that had happened. How could she ever forgive me, how would she ever look at me again, without feeling disgust toward me…

I knew that the words in the diary had broke her heart, they had to have. And yet, she was sitting there so calmly, and so gently whispering to me. I watched her as she stood up to leave my room, as she started to turn away from me, she turned and grabbed my face in her hands, and took my face up to look at hers' " **I promise you this will never happen again"**. I just sat there with my mouth open and tears streaming from my face… So many questions I was asking myself, "What would he do if she told him she knew?... Would he send her away from us, have her put away? How would I fight him if he tried?" For someone still no more than a young teen, I was facing a lot of worries.

He didn't come near me, didn't speak to me for nearly two days, and though I should have been relieved that he wasn't bothering me, I felt this impending doom... Mother even acted as though she was punishing me for doing wrong.

Well I had done wrong, I had run away…I can imagine it had scared her to death, worrying over me, not knowing where I was. I could only imagine that she went in search of the diary to get a clue as to my whereabouts...only to find the diary...what she must have felt when she opened and read it. It had to have been so hard for her to understand, to swallow...that her daughter was being molested.

Two days must have seemed long enough to my Father to come back into my room. That night I felt the pull on the covers, the eerie feeling I had felt so many times before... signaling me to hold tight to my blankets...Once again he was naked below the waist, ready to take care of his nasty needs and throw his evidence away in the tissue paper like he had so many times in my life.

"What in the hell do you think you are doing?.. Get your pants on now, you Son-Of-A-Bitch"...my Mother's scream could be heard through out the house, waking my sister as she lay in the other bed in my room.

After all these years of being tortured, my sister who couldn't be woke by a bomb...was awakened this night. She could see exactly what my Mother was screaming about. My Father without his boxer's...caught red handed...trying desperately to put them on and giving some sort of half-attempt of an excuse.

CHAPTER SEVEN

The sexual abuse would end when I was sixteen years old. No way he could have my Mother put away when my sister had awaken and seen him too. No way he could lie his way out of this with all of us knowing his dirty secret. It was all over…the threats, the games, the torture I felt to have to go to bed at night…

Most of my privileges would be given back to me, though this did not make my Father the least bit happy. Life in the household had appeared almost normal as early as the next morning. No one spoke of what had happened the night before. There was no shouting, no angry words. I did not have a clue what was said in the deep of the night, but I can imagine she might have threatened to go to our Church with his actions, and I assumed that the voices during the night had remained hushed in order for Jack, my brother, to not be alerted as to what had taken place.

Oh, he never got easier to live with, he still was just as cold and uncaring as ever, still just as threatening to me about everything I did. I walked on pins and needles around him and he let me know as often as he could what a low down sorry piece of white trash Chase was.

He hated him with every fiber of his being, and yet he still drove up and down the road if I went to spend the night with someone. I was getting smarter though, If he wanted me in bed by a certain time when I spent the night somewhere, then we would have all the lights out by that time, and continue to laugh and tell stories by the light of the moon or a night light . I guess the saying is true - . "Where there is a will, there is a way."

I was also allowed to date again, once weekly with Chase. Of course my Father hated that too... but Mother over looked what he wanted and saw nothing wrong with my dating. I enjoyed the freedom almost like a young adult in so many ways, and yet...the innocence of most 16 year olds could never compare to what I had lived through in my young life.

Never were there signs of affection between my Mother and Father. There hadn't been in a long time. We, the children, had been used to hearing him put our Mother and her lack of abilities down in front of us, the people at Church, or even someone he knew at a gas station. He didn't care if Mother was standing there, he got enjoyment out of ridiculing her.

She became more bitter at him with each passing day, and he would put more threats on her. I knew it, could feel it. He enjoyed saying cruel things about her and then laughing about it... just like he had done to me most of my life.

One afternoon, my Father told us that he was taking Mother somewhere and would be back in a little while. We really didn't know what had happened, and he didn't tell us. What we didn't know was that he had taken her to a Psychiatric hospital outside of town. We didn't know what had happened to bring it on, if our Mother had tried to hurt herself or overdose on her medication's again. He had put her in there, he said to the family, for her own good.

I didn't believe it ,even if someone had shown me positive proof that something was wrong with Mother, I still would believe he did it to punish her and keep her quiet about the things she knew. He did it to show her that he could carry out his threats. He did it to show her that if she ever told a soul what she knew about him, he would have her put away for a long time. He had threatened it, now he was proving it. She spent a little over a week there, but from all the terrible stories I have heard, she was living in a hell on earth, with people so much worse than she could ever be, purely psychotic people.

When she came home, she was again quiet and withdrawn. I hated him, and no longer felt I needed to respect him in anyway. Aunt Margaret would get on me every chance she got for being disrespectful of him. I didn't care. Who was she to tell me to disrespect a man that had molested me most of my life anyway? So when he would say things to her just to hurt her, I would stand up against him. I came to her defense constantly. I would fight with him openly. He was telling the family now that I was talking back to him, he would punish me for it... make me look like I was a the worst teen that ever walked, to the family. I didn't care anymore what he said or did. He could send me away, but after what my Mother looked like when she had come home from that hospital, I swore I would see him in hell before she went back there again.

Unfortunately, as much as I thought I was stronger and more determined and could take on the world against him... there was still a weakness within me, I could still be bullied by him. I had thought of suicide many times.. writing a letter to my Aunt Elda, my Mother's sister... and in the letter I would tell her the whole sordid details of what had taken place. If anything happened to me I wanted Mother to be protected against him. I didn't want to hide the secrets anymore, I wanted him to pay, and pay dearly. Only, I didn't have the strength to just go up to a family member and tell them what I knew, what I felt...I was so afraid that no one would care or believe me.

One afternoon with yet another bitter argument about Chase, and my being a worthless slut, I quietly went into my parents room, climbed up on my Mother's Cedar Chest and reached to the back of the upper closet to retrieve the gun. I truly had in my mind that I was going to end the pain once and for all. The note had been written…there would be no more fights, no more living with the past. No more nightmares as I slept, of what had happened to me for so many years. No more trying to remain strong, when I didn't have the strength too. No more trying to gain courage when I felt I had used it all up through out the years. Chase could go on and live his life with someone more deserving…just one bullet would stop it all.

I looked at the shiny revolver - I knew how to shoot it, and decided that my mouth would be the perfect place to put it. At that moment, between here on earth and just letting it all go, my Mother walked in. She grabbed the gun from my hand and sat down next to me, "This is not the answer" she said softly. I just burst into tears, much needed tears... years of abuse and hatred filled tears. I held on to her for dear life.

I don't know if I understood why I had not went ahead with my plan or if the tears had just brought with it some of the relief I needed…whatever change had taken place I was not certain of.. but I put dying on hold.

Chase and I continue to date. The new found "petting" had become a routine part of our dates out with each other. I felt like an angel in his arms, I needed him to touch me, touched by someone with gentle hands and a gentle voice.

I was so extremely shy about my body, still knew that if he ever saw me naked he would not stay with me. No matter how much he tried to convince me otherwise, I knew it was only a matter of time before he found someone better and would move on.

My confidence was to slow in coming. Something that I desperately needed…but Chase, without even realizing it, was making me feel more like a woman everyday and less like a frightened little girl. The touches to my arms, legs were becoming easier to allow. His kisses becoming more enjoyable and some of my guard was being let down, the pain of yesterday seeming to slowly fade away.

Friends of Chase's were picking on me about being "little miss virgin." They would leave condoms where we could find them. Chase always came to my defense, and amidst my anger would always comfort me and tell me we would be together when the time was right. There was nothing wrong with waiting until marriage if that was what I wanted.

Jennifer and her many talks with me regarding sex is what finally made the transition for me, helping me to turn the corner. Chase and I had been together for over two years now, I was 16. I had wanted to be with Chase for a long time but my fears kept my mouth shut, my inner soul closed off. I wanted to give myself to him, I really wanted him to be my first…I just wasn't sure just how I would go about it. I was also afraid of what the day would bring, would it be regret on his part?

Thinking about the event became almost as important as anything else - It was all I could think of. Finally one evening, I approached the subject with Chase, I looked right into his eyes as if I had suddenly become bold and said, "I don't want to be a virgin anymore," - the look in his eyes told me that I had shocked him. I expected him to start making plans.

Instead I was the one that was shocked when he said to me "I don't think your as ready as you think you are, we will know when the time is right." Time is right? I had thought to myself.

"Now is the time before I lose my cool." I was young, and I knew I was ready for the next step.

I had held him, touched him, stroked him…I wanted to learn more. And the teacher wasn't giving in as readily as I had hoped for. It was years before I realized that he was just trying to make sure I was in a good place before we went any further. He had wanted to be sure it was what I really wanted and not because I was pressured by his friends or mine.....

CHAPTER EIGHT

Sex was all that I could think about. With everyone else enjoying it and me having no idea or no comment to make, I was far behind them. I am not sure if it was the sexual act itself that pushed me or if I just wanted to feel normal like my friends. I wanted to be able to tell them I was a woman too. But, Chase was not budging...so, I decided to push him into it.

Jennifer and I came up with a plan one night while spending the night at her house. I would lure Chase to my bed, well.. not exactly my bed, but her boyfriend's brother's bed. Her new boyfriend, Brian Davis had a cool car, a GTO, better know by us as a 'Goat'. He also had parents that went on vacation and left the two brother's home to go to school. Brian had the run of the house, and he and Jennifer would go there during those days when the parents were gone, and make love until curfew. So.. she and I decided to tell Chase that we were going skating the following weekend on a double date.

Brian and Jennifer picked me up first, and then went to Chase's house and retrieved him. There he was, as handsome as ever, with his skates in tow. He immediately wanted to know where my skates were, we all just kind of giggled and put him off about his question. As we pulled into Brian's driveway though, he wanted to know why we were there. Well, being the young scared woman that I was, I proceeded nervously to tell him we were not going skating. We were here together, to make love for the first time. There was no more excuses Chase could come up with, no more reasons as to why I should wait. I guess he realized my mind was made up.

Sex for the first time was by no means what I had imagined. I had trouble undressing in front of him and insisted that the lights be off…I was grateful for the darkness. The petting and kissing had went well, up to the point of the actual act itself. When the moment of truth arrived, I had no idea that my legs could become so stiff like a board and I am sure Chase had no idea just how much strength I had in them.

But with him talking me through, trying to get me to relax against my profound fear, my asking stupid questions like "are you in yet?", his reassurances over and over to calm down…the initial pain that I hadn't expected…and then the overwhelming feeling that I belong to someone. We had made it through. I came away with a feeling like I had never known before. I felt as though I had given an important part of myself to him, and he was treating me as if I had too. I felt security I had never known, and beautiful beyond words - even if it were for this six hour stretch of time.

After finding the love that I did with Chase at such a young age, the poetry I had been writing most of my life was coming full circle. No longer was I writing about the darkness I saw before my eyes, but now I was writing love sonnets, love poems, saving them all in a book instead of throwing them away. It was my new outlet, and I enjoyed saving these poems and even wrote a book of them for my Mother's Birthday.

My Father was still there in my in my life, like a cancer that comes and goes... still hating Chase and no matter what, Chase could do no right. My Mother would be hospitalized several more times from drug over-doses, there was another Electric Shock treatment, and many trips to the psychiatrist. It was during one of those visits that Mom asked me to go with her.

She drove us there. I didn't know why she needed me to go, but I went anyway. During her session, I was asked to come in and join the Doctor. My Mother spilled out to the Doctor what she had found in my diary, and what she had caught my Father doing. The Therapist asked me several questions, all of which were very personal and I hated having to respond to the answers in front of my Mother, it was so embarrassing. The psychiatrist said that I should be in counseling as well…but I didn't want to have any part of telling someone about what had been so private and disgusting to talk about. When we left the office Mother asked me to never tell my Father that I had been in the session, or what had been talked about…and I never did.

On the good days with Mother we could laugh and joke and play just like it had been so many years before. Chase would come over and play the guitar and sing for her. She loved Chase, and he loved her just as much. He would come to dinner at our house and then play his guitar…all of which chewed away at my Father, and made him even angrier at my Mother for allowing him to be there.

On Christmas Day of my 16th year, Chase bought me an engagement ring and proudly presented it to me at my house. I accepted it, and called everyone I knew with the news that I had been so lucky as to have Chase want to marry me…someone like me.

My Mother was happy for me. Ah, but my father was not. He laid his foot down firmly, I would not be allowed to marry this "sorry white trash" - not now, not ever. I would not be allowed to ever date him again if he had his way about it. It would start yet another argument between my Mother and Father - angry and verbal.

My Father was forbidding the marriage, he demanded I give the ring back. Finally to stop the war going on in the house, and give my Mother some peace against the fighting, I gave in and told my Father if he would let me continue to see Chase, I would give the ring back. He agreed with that and the fighting stopped.

Chase and I then agreed that I would hide the ring in my purse and wear it when we were out together or while I was at school. Together, we made the decision that I would finish school and then get married as soon as I had graduated. I was in Cosmetology at that time too, and needed to complete that class as well. I would graduate in June, and right after graduation we would say our 'I do's'.

Father didn't let it go, just couldn't make life easier. The fights continued over my dating anyway. The arguments continued over Chase being allowed in the house or even calling me on the phone. He would find something wrong with him every chance he got, only spurring me to want to be with him more. He would go so far in his revenge that he would accuse him of robbing houses down the street, even though we showed him proof that Chase was in school when the robberies took place. He just couldn't let go. He would make it known every chance he got that he would not allow me to marry Chase at any point before I became an adult on my own.

But Chase was my security, he kept me safe. He held me when I became angry over all that was going on at home. I needed desperately to be with him and hold tightly to him.

One night in the midst of one of our conversations together, we devised our own plan. If my Father was going to stand in the way of us getting married, and of Chase's protection of me from the war zone I lived in all the time…then we would devise our own plan. I would get pregnant, and then Father would have to let us marry.

CHAPTER NINE

Marriage to Chase meant freedom from my life at home, freedom from the pain, my protection. I was already known by most of the family members as the "Black Sheep" because of the stories my Father had told them about me....so getting pregnant, would be just one more terrible sin I would do to add to that name. Marriage would give me my independence, and all the nightmares I had lived with would soon be gone.

It took no time at all for me to become pregnant. The next month to be exact. Unfortunately, it did not come together as we had planned. Nothing like what we had anticipated. Chase and I sat down with my parents and told them. My Father without uttering a word got up and left the room, when he returned he had his pistol in hand and walked over to Chase and put it to his head and demanded him out of his house that instant. Chase did as he was instructed to do, for fear of his life. But I believed to also protect me from being in the line of fire should Chase have fought against him.

As soon as Chase was out of the door, my Mother with a look of contempt across her face and hatred in her eyes, came over to me and started lashing out at me. She hit me, over and over again, hit me hard about the face with her fist. Hit my arms. She tried to hit me in the stomach, I held my hands and legs firm to my waist in a balled up position to protect my unborn child , protect this child that lay innocent and fresh inside me from the pure blunt of anger I was receiving.

It had never dawned on me to fight back, after all she was my Mother. I looked up and saw that my Father was just standing there, watching it all happen. A smile firmly pressed on his lips. He would watch the whole thing take place and never lift a finger to stop the blows to my face and body. I was as powerless as I had ever been in my life..submissive. Again, I felt somehow I deserved every hit I took. I had disgraced my Mother and my family by this, and this was my punishment...

In the middle of all that was happening, the police were in the house and stopping my Mother. I can not tell you when they came in the door, who let them in or if they had just barged in...but they were there. Chase had called them from the neighbor's house, he had never actually left, just moved his car down the road and had walked back up to the house and heard what was happening and called them. The police wanted me to press charges, but I refused. She was my Mother.

The police asked if there was somewhere I could go, a neighbor, a friend, a family member. They told me to pack a bag. I thought of Jennifer..she would come if I called her.. she would be there for me.

Through the tears and with the police guarding me, I called Jennifer and tried to explain quickly that I needed to stay at her house. She knew what ever happened had been serious by the sound of my voice. She then talked to her Mother, and within several minutes was there to pick me up. Chase waited until after Jennifer arrived, helped to load my things, then told me everything would be alright from then on out...I believed him. The Police had waited too, not allowing my Father or Mother to speak to me, or allowed them to get near me. To this day I have no idea what the police might have said to them after I left, and have no idea what Chase might have said to my Father either...

Jennifer's family was already in bed when we arrived. She had woke her Mother up to tell her bits of what she knew, and ask permission to come and get me, so that when her family woke in the morning they would understand why I was there at their home. Jennifer and I made up cots in the dining room to sleep on, as her Uncle and Aunt were visiting from North Florida.

I was too tired to think about, worry about why my face hurt so bad, why my neck and arms hurt to move, or if I had bruises or not - Jennifer hadn't said. I just explained what had happened, she had already known I was pregnant. She already knew our plans to get married...I cried in her arms for a little bit, and then we both were so worn out we just went to sleep. Tomorrow I would face whatever happened. Tonight, I needed sleep.

Morning came very early, I was awaken by whispers of people in the kitchen. Jennifer's Mom, Celia, and her Aunt Susan were talking, and though I could not hear it clearly, I knew they were talking about me. I thought maybe her Mom was mad that I was there, that she was voicing her opinion. I was afraid to get out of my bed to find out. I could hear the whispered curse words, but could not make out the conversation. I waited for Jennifer to wake up and lead the way to the kitchen...

Jennifer's Mom was not speaking angrily about me, no...she had peeked in on us that morning early and had seen my face as I slept. She was voicing her opinion of my parents. Of how they could have done this to me, their child

Celia's eyes started to tear up and she let out a gasp when I walked into the brightly lit kitchen. Choking on her words as she spoke, she was clearly angry, and verbally so. It was the first time for me that an adult had ever sided with me like that, it was such a strange feeling that I was not sure what to say or do, so I just stood there silently and listened as Celia angrily spoke more toward her sister in law then to anyone else in the room.

CHAPTER TEN

Over the next several days, Celia fought several battles for me. She had spoken roughly to my Father when he had come to the door demanding to speak to me. She had not allowed him into her house and told him he had done enough damage. Celia was a small woman, and my Father big and burly.

I suspect it was the first time he had ever had a woman stand up against him totally, especially one as small as she was, but she was feisty and she stood her ground. She protected me at every turn that was made. I enjoyed this feeling, it had a warmth to it, it was a feeling like I really did matter in this world, and that even though I was young…I mattered to an adult…to Jennifer's Mom, a woman that had not raised me, but yet was willing to stick her neck out to protect me.

The next few days would be spent in arguments regarding me getting an abortion. My parents would call, demanding to speak to me, only to get into a war of words with Celia. My parents wanted me to have an abortion, something I was totally against, something Celia was against. Countless phone calls, countless trips to the door to try and bully her. She would not give in. My parents had it in their mind that if I stayed pregnant, I would disgrace the family name. And back in those days a parent could have the abortion done against the teen's will.

Unfortunately, my parents made two fatal errors in their plight to have the abortion done though. They had called the pastor of our Church, Rev. Kilter, and had called my favorite

Aunt, my Mother's sister Elda. The mistake that my parents made was not finding out the view point on abortion that the Reverend, my Aunt and Grandmother might have had.

I was told of the meeting that would take place the following afternoon, by Celia…she had told me not to worry about it, that if they started anything she would boot them out of her house. No one would be able to push me into an abortion, she would see to it. From the moment the meeting had started it was clear that no one in the room was impressed with either of my parents. Starting from when I answered the door and Grandma saw my make-up clad face, that still clearly showed the bruises through it "Who did this to you?" I remember her saying.

I didn't have to answer as Aunt Elda answered for me "Who do you think did this to her?"

I clearly remember the change to my Grandma's face, the gritting of her teeth as she touched my arm and walked past me. I had been Grandma's little girl for so many years when I was younger, until my Father and his lies about me being a problem child started to drive a wedge between us. I had been harmed, hurt. To say the least she was not pleased…

You might say this was the beginning of the end about the abortion issue. My Aunt Elda went off in front of everyone in the group about the fact that my Mother and Father had slept together prior to marriage…and how could they judge me for doing the same sinful thing…how could they doubt this might happen when Chase and I had been dating exclusively for three years?? Aunt Elda asked my Mother "Who beat you up when you were sleeping around, Sandy? Who hit you Harold when you were running around with women all over town?" No answer came from them, but I could clearly see the shame in my Mother's eyes. I wasn't the only one being punished now, my parents were…

It did not stop with my Aunt or my Grandma, but the Reverend had a say as well. "How could they as good Christian people want to even consider killing an unborn child? Yes…we had sinned in sleeping together prior to marriage, but my parents were trying to force their daughter into murder…and if they succeeded…they would no longer be allowed in his Church…" I had no idea. First Celia had stood by me, then my Aunt and my Grandma and now even the Reverend.

Rev. Kilter asked what Chase and I wanted to do about the position we were in, and we told him we wanted to marry and have the baby. He agreed, but said the marriage should take place within the next couple of weeks so that it would keep some of the gossip down about the whole event. Everyone agreed with the plan except my parents. They were against it, and since I had just turned 17 in October , they would not sign for me to get married. My grandmother spoke up with that; she demanded my Mother or Father sign or she would pay for it to go before the court and let the Judge do it.

I was to be married in under two weeks, a Saturday in February, the 21st day to be exact. Thank goodness for Jennifer's mom. She found her other daughter's prom dresses and we decided on a light blue chiffon, floor length gown. She went out and bought the material for my veil and put it together. She bought the corsages for Chase and his best man, James. Jennifer got one of her prom dresses to wear. Celia decorated the Church…I felt both honored by Celia and yet a little guilty because she had to do this for me. My parents were kind enough to buy the cake and finger foods for the wedding. My Father was forced to walk me down the aisle.

The morning of the wedding, Celia and Jennifer helped me to get dressed and apply my make up to hide the now yellow and green bruises to my face and arms. I should have been nervous, this was my wedding day, yet I wasn't. I guess I was so happy to be breaking away from the pain and frustrations of living at home that there was no time for nervousness.

I walked down the aisle in the blue chiffon dress and held my head high. As expected, my parents played the perfect part with sweet smiles of joy. Pictures were taken...a smile to everyone's faces...I, the glowing bride with my handsome groom...what could have been more perfect...

CHAPTER ELEVEN

Now one would think, well, at least I did…that this would be the end of the book...right? After all, isn't this the end of the fairy tale finally…suffering girl meets, falls in love with, and marries her White Knight. They live together in beautiful harmony. They grow old and watch the grandchildren grow up….ahhhh…but only if it were that easy.

The Nightmare's do not end simply because you leave the nightlight on…..

THEY ECHO…

Pregnancy did me justice and I had bountiful amounts of energy. I was learning how to experiment with my husband in all that marriage had to do with, including sex. We were learning to enjoy our new found freedom, on our own, young and free. I was going to night school to finish up and get my Diploma, and during the day finishing up my Cosmetology course. Chase was working full-time, he had worked from the first day we met, so it had been easy for him to go from part- time to full-time. We had our little apartment, his old car, a few pieces of furniture…we thought we had it all.

There was just a few flaws in this new marriage...I could not, no matter how hard Chase tried, be naked in front of him. I had to be clothed in something, even if it was a sheet. Oh he tried to pull the sheet off a few times to expose me, but with all my strength I would fight him off till I won out. Marriage had not changed my fears regarding my body, and Chase was getting nowhere in seeing what his wife actually looked like under her clothes. I wouldn't allow him in the bathroom when I bathed or anything else…the phobia was to strong.

Chase knew that I had to face my fear on my own, but he was hoping an accidental pull on the sheet would expose me, would make me realize that I wasn't as hideous as I believed myself to be.

There had also been times in the marriage and deep into a sexual act with my husband that without notice, my Father's face would appear in front of me, harassing me...the same face I had seen for years as it had come into my room. I would immediately panic and push Chase off of me. He never got angry, always seemed to understand. He would whisper to me over and over till it got through my head that the demon was not there. It was Chase. He would force me to look at him and would repeat over and over: " Look at me…it's me…your safe…your safe." I heard those words so much that when ever I was frightened about anything…I would use those words over and over in my mind.

To the outside world I looked like I was growing and maturing with the added responsibilities of life. My grades were high on everything, I did in night school and in Cosmetology. But…Chase knew it was no more than a smoke screen. I was a little girl, scared and afraid, and that I needed Chase to cling to as my sense of security.

It had taken a little while, and had taken me realizing that when my Mother hit me that day, she did it not to hurt me so much as to lash out the only way she knew how. I had been her only friend in that house, the only one that truly knew what was going on. Now she was left to Him and the four walls around her. So it had been her fear of being alone in that house with Him that had caused her to do what she did. And...without realizing it, I had been selfish in wanting out, and not thinking of the consequences my Mother would have to endure.

My Mother and I did make up. We started going out to lunch together and looking for baby clothes. She was accepting the fact that she would be a Grandma soon...even looking forward to the baby's birth. I was glad to have my Mother back and so very glad that she still loved me.

I graduated from school and Cosmetology just short of the babies birth... and as soon as the baby was born I had to take my last exam in Cosmetology in Winterhaven.

That early fall, just two weeks short of my 18th birthday, a beautiful fair- skinned, rosy cheeked baby girl came into our lives; we named her Sierra. She was perfect in every way. She didn't have much hair, so was called a tow- head baby. From the moment I looked into her precious eyes, I knew that I would protect her at all cost. My Mother and I bonded even closer now with this sweet little child. Chase and I grew even closer which to most people was thought to be odd with all the added responsibility at our young ages. We had created something from love, something that was a part of both of us, something I needed in my life to fill the void.

Before we could even get this new adventure going well, another daughter was born, 11 months later, three months prematurely. This little girl looked so much like her dark haired, dark skinned father it was amazing; we decided to give her the name Hannah. Because of her early birth she had health problems, mostly with her lungs. We were so afraid we were going to lose her, and even did for a short time early on. The doctor brought her back to us, her heart and lungs working again.

They rushed her to the Children's Hospital. I had been

through a Cesarean with her, and so I was rather weak, but with Chase by my side we willed our baby to live…We decided that when this baby was born I would have my tubes tied, we had all the family we could ever want. Our second daughter came home to us at six weeks old and a whopping 4lbs 11 ounces, and though the doctor's said she wouldn't make it to five years old, we believed that with love and protection she would. Nonetheless….we had our family, complete.

Chase and I were so close then, it was almost as if at times we could read each other's minds. Friends thought it was eerie that I seemed to know what he needed. There we were, he at 20 and me almost 19, with two children to care for. Trying to hold down two jobs, and work around sitters. Besieged with the bills that were way over our heads at times. Struggling with life.

The pregnancies had left me with stretch marks and a little added weight…so even with my happy marriage, my self esteem was lower than ever. I believed now that one day I would come home and Chase would be gone. My Father, being who he was only added fuel to the fire. He would call constantly and tell me that one family member or another had found Chase with another woman.

And…the more that my Father called with this news, the tighter the dependency on Chase became. I took on more roles around the house to please him. Started laying his clothes out to wear to work and running his bath water for when he came home in the evenings. I wanted Chase to be the happiest man in the world. He had married this tawdry girl, he had made her feel safe from her Father….had helped turn this girl into a young woman…I owed him all that I could do for him. I over looked my Father's warnings of other women, and I held on tightly to Chase.

My Mother came over and floored me when she said she

was divorcing my Father. She wanted to know if she and my sister could come and live with us until she got her life together, and then she would move out to a place on her own. Of course we said she could. My God…I knew what she had been through with that Monster she had for a husband, I didn't have to ask her what happened to finally change her mind and make her want to leave him….but I was happy that she would be able to break away from his cruelty and begin to live a normal life.

CHAPTER TWELVE

The obsession over Chase began…the calls from my Father continued, wearing away at my self- reliance. I started watching his actions, asking questions of him constantly…expecting the worst to be said. If he came home with flowers for me, I knew that there had to be another reason besides his love for me.

The worst moment of my life was yet to be realized…. I had the day off, and decided to take the children over to see their Grandmother. She played with them, chased after them, held them on her lap.. and we had chatted for a long time. I watched as my Father and sister, Gale, left to go to Church. My brother had already left for work and it was getting late . I knew I needed to get home so I left shortly after they did. I kissed my Mother on the cheek, she kissed the children…and I left hoping to beat Chase home so that I could fix dinner.

The call came in about one- and-a- half hours after I had gotten home, it was my Father…. "Mother has tried to commit suicide again, get to the house quickly" was all I heard. I dropped the phone.. Chase talked to my Father on the phone and within minutes we were on the road, me begging God for her to be alright, once again. Chase holding my hand, and trying to keep me calm even though he already knew from the conversation with my Father that it wasn't going to be alright.

We left the children off with Chase's Mother and got to the house to find police cars and an ambulance already there.

My Mother was dead. My Father told us that when he

returned home from church, he had found the house dark and found that my Mother had shot herself. He had walked into the room and in his shock, he said he had accidently picked up the gun and then lay it back down.

A woman that knew nothing about guns, had put a bullet in it and had shot herself in her right temple and killed herself.

The police ruled it a suicide....

I had loved her so much, Chase had loved her almost as much as I did. Both of us had come to realize long ago that my Mother was a victim just like I had been...just differently. She had given up....for whatever reason had decided not leave him, I assumed...decided that death was the way out.

But, Chase believed that she had not tried to take her life, he was sure that my Father had something to do with it. When he first brought it up, I didn't have the strength to argue the point. I had lost my mother, she had left me alone, and in my mind did not love me enough to stay and fight against all of her problems. I didn't want to hear what he had to say. My friend, my Mother, the Grandmother of my children was gone...and that's all I could focus on..

The days would come and fill me with guilt because I should have gotten her out of there, I should have made her stay with me the day she came to talk about the divorce. I should have never allowed her to go home. She must have been at the lowest point in her life. My whole world felt like it was tumbling in, I was sad and depressed. I stopped working. I started sleeping longer, going to bed earlier. And...becoming so angry at God for taking the wrong parent. The more depressed and withdrawn I became, the more Chase stayed at the bars and drank, and the more we fought.

Chase had begun working for another company and they would go to the bars after work, he had drank once and a while before this…but now it was a nightly ritual. The longer he stayed out, the more mistrustful I became. The more obsessed I became, the more Chase stayed in the bars, the more he would drink…and the more my Father would call about someone seeing him with another woman. I would call Jennifer and talk to her almost nightly. I could not hold on to Chase, and he was losing sight of the girl I once was.

He would come home and I would suffocate him and accuse him of things that he had to keep defensively repeating, he had not done…Where we once could understand each other without words, now we were not able to understand anything. Chase would come home drunk and refer to my Father as a murderer…and that one day he would get his revenge on him. I would have to battle him over it. I had lost my hold. I could not fight the drinking...I didn't know how to fight to keep my own life above water, let alone fight what was happening between us…

The fights over absolutely nothing escalated, the doors slamming around us. He would come home from a drinking binge and be hateful and angry toward me. We no longer could communicate. He would spend the night away from home and I would believe he was in another woman's arms. I watched as my White Knight was slipping away from my finger tips.

One afternoon with his Uncle Fred in tow, he walked into the house and started packing his clothing. He was silent, hard; his face tight. I kept asking him what he was doing, he would not answer me. I grabbed at his arm to turn him toward me and he gave me the most dreadful look I had ever seen, like he wanted me dead. I could not in my mind figure out what had happened, but he was leaving me just the same. He walked out the door without uttering a word.

Now I was not only grieving over my Mother, but I was

grieving for Chase as well. My world felt like it was spiraling out of control and I couldn't figure out how to stop it.

We did try to reconcile a couple of times, and for a few weeks it would work and then deteriorate again rapidly…our marriage finally ending with the ultimate slamming of the door.

Our marriage of five years was over with, the boy that I had started dating when I was 14 and whom I married at 17 had walked out of my life and with him….my security.

CHAPTER THIRTEEN

Days on end I would lay there and look at the ceiling, days on end Jennifer would try to console me or listen to me over the phone. Other friends would show up at the door, wanting to help. Each thought I just need to get on with life, that it would be much easier to let go of Chase that way.

Chase's brother Derek and his wife Sara had been living with us when the last break up had occurred, so he had to hear the rambling as well. Thankfully, Derek and Sara stayed on after Chase left and helped to fill the void that was left in my life. Sara and I became good friends during this time.

A friend of both Chase's and mine, Rick Rodgers, started coming over and sitting with me in the evenings. He would comfort me and tell me everything would be alright. He told me that he would be there for me whenever I needed him.

Days went by with Rick coming by every evening. He floored me when one evening out of the blue, he said he loved me. He told me he would protect me. I guess I needed to hear those words. Needed to feel like someone cared about me. I just had wished it was Chase that was doing the talking. To say I was confused would have been an understatement. I still loved and missed Chase, I still ached for him. I wanted back what we had lost..

Derek and Sara would listen to my whining, being so loyal and understanding. One night after a long talk with Derek and him telling me it was time to move on with my life ,that the marriage was over…I went to my bedroom with Rick in tow and had sex with him.

I felt so guilty afterwards, I had given something that had belonged to Chase for so many years, away to someone else. Something special was now gone and Rick had it. It had not been everything I had hoped for, and certainly nothing like what Chase and I had shared in bed…but then every man is different. It had hurt to have sex with Rick, something I had never experienced with Chase, but I chalked it up to nervousness and let it go.

My feelings became even more confused. I knew I could not turn back now, knew that no matter what…when Chase found out what I had done, he would hate me, hate me forever. Probably as much as I hated myself…

I filed for the divorce, it was the first anniversary of my Mother's death the day I signed the papers…a lot of terrible things had happened in that year since her death….it only stood to make the matters worse…tear me apart even more.

Within two months I was living with Rick. He said he would take care of me and the children. He was gentle toward me, understanding. He told me he would be the security I needed. I believed he would be just that. He had been a long time friend to me, so I had hoped that perhaps that friendship might be able to grow into something else. The longing for Chase was getting a little easier to bear. I could put him out of my mind, unless I saw him somewhere or heard his name mentioned.

Rick asked me to marry him, and I told him I still loved Chase. He had said he would learn to live with it, and that it was worth trying, I could learn to love him. He had done so much for me already, had given me back some of the secure feeling I had lost when my Mother had died and then Chase had left. I felt I needed to give him something in return. No one said don't do it, I am sure it was because I finally had a smile to my face and was getting on with my life.

One afternoon, shortly before the marriage was to take place, Chase came by the apartment complex we lived in. He asked if he could speak with me. I said we could and we went outside to talk. He wanted us to get together again, try one more time to make our lives work together.

God, I wanted too....I didn't even know why...but I wanted to.. I knew though, that I couldn't do it. I had in my mind destroyed the last thread of our marriage when I had slept with Rick. I couldn't turn back now. I belonged to this man now. I couldn't bear to tell Chase that. I hadn't faced most of it or understood my actions myself. I knew that because legally Chase and I had been married, though living apart, I had committed adultery. Chase would never forgive me for that. I told Chase the best way I knew how, that we no longer had a future, I was marrying Rick. He kissed me lightly on the cheek and I went back upstairs to the apartment, and cried for hours. R ick and I were married. Chase moved up north and went into the Army. No letters, no pictures, no calls to the children from him. He had moved on with his life completely and apparently had no room in his life even for the children. It wasn't until many years later that letters started resurfacing that one of his sister's had in her possession, that told a different story. For what ever reason, she had gotten them and held on to them and never brought them over for the kids or I to see....

To say that the marriage with Rick was going well, would be a complete lie. I didn't know who's fault it was exactly, mine or his...but there was trouble from the start. He had told me before we married that he had understood how I felt, said he could wait for me to love him. In actuality he had taken back everything he had said.

It killed him that I cared for someone else, hated that he couldn't break through to me..and most of all hated that I had not fallen in love with him yet. He was jealous and possessive of my every move. I couldn't go anywhere unless it was with his family. He started governing how I wore my hair and the type of clothing I wore. He wouldn't allow me to wear the clothing that I found comfortable, but instead would spend great deals of money on clothing that I hated from the mall near us. Suddenly I was dressing in the best fashions. There was no time to visit my own friends…only time to be with his family which had become an almost daily occurrence.

If I had been dependent on Chase, I was even worse with Rick. He told me the moves I could and could not make. He refused to let me go to work. I didn't argue too much with him about it, I knew I was never right. If he got verbal with me, If he got angry at me, then it was because I deserved it. After all, he had married me knowing I loved someone else….he deserved to be treated with respect for taking care of me and the children.

The biggest defect to our marriage was the size of Rick's penis. The more we had sex, the more I hurt inside. I would try and endure it, but sometimes I just couldn't handle the pain. When the pain got too great, I went to the doctor and was told that Rick was tearing the ligaments around the cervix and that is why I had so much pain. The doctor told Rick he would have to insert half way, that my body could not take the abuse anymore. But, Rick would not change, and sex became a chore rather than an adventure for a couple to share.

Finally I got to were I could not perform at all, no matter how much I thought he might have deserved it. Rick nevertheless was a man and he deserved his wife in bed with him, and I was that wife. I would try to accommodate him, only to find myself actually getting sick to my stomach. He would get angry at me...but the pain of the sexual act far out weighed the pain of his anger.

I started taking tranquilizers that the Doctor had prescribed for my nerves: my hands shook, I had constant headaches, I was always sick to my stomach. One night after taking my usual dose of Librium I went to bed and fell asleep. I don't know how long I had slept...but the searing red hot pain in my lower back woke me up with a snap...

Rick was taking what he wanted anally. He had been told time and time again I could not handle that position. He was taking it anyway. Without thinking I hit him as hard as my fist could hit, calling him as many names as I could think of at the top of my lungs.

I got out of the bed and stumbled to get to my robe. In my eyes I had been anally raped whether we were married or not. All of my childhood rearing up and slapping me in the face, no matter what I thought I owed him, in my eyes he was no better than my Father.

Whatever I was hoping I could accomplish in making Rick happy, was over now; he had abused me in a way I never wanted to be abused again. The marriage was over....in less than a year.

CHAPTER FOURTEEN

I was on my own again, really for the first time in my life, and very scared of being out in this world by myself. I had went from home to being with Chase, to the break up and right into Rick's home. I had never been on my own, making my own decisions.

A friend of mine from school came to my aid this time, Cory Jacobs. A sweet, sensitive woman with a young son, she was beautiful and had the attention of many mens eyes. She offered me a place to stay with my children. She became my security and my protection. I was to pay half the bills when I got on my feet. She kept everyone at bay for a short time..it was just the children, the house, and us.

Chase was living in Indiana at this time with his second wife, Macy. Somewhere during the time I was at Cory's, he separated from her and came back to Florida. He found out I was also separated and getting a divorce, and looked me up again.

We started to see each other, to date; it felt like the old times. Full of sparkle and hope for the future, everything seemed to be going well for us. He didn't seem to be drinking like he used to… he seemed like the old Chase I remembered so well. He told me that he has never loved another woman that way that he has loved me all of those years, and I believed him. I had felt the same way, no one had come close to the love I had carried for him. I think that he has forgiven me for the marriage to Rick…I am not sure he understands…we do not discuss what happened at any great length. I am just glad to have him in my arms again. To have the children's Dad home with them again….

I go to the Doctor because I have missed two periods, I am sure it is something to do with hormones or something internal due to the abuse to my Cervix. I expect the Doctor to run some test, which he does….I am very shocked to learn through those test that I test positive for pregnancy. I argue with him that it is impossible, It has been years since I had a tubal Ligation done. He reruns the test and then does a pelvic exam on me…there is no mistake, I am six weeks pregnant.

"God's will to the tenth power"…I think to myself as I drive home from the Doctor's. "Chase and my second chance at happiness"…I tell Cory. I am on edge and nervously excited to tell Chase that the impossible has happened and we have a baby on the way. The heavens are shining down on us. Maybe this will be the son I have wanted for a few years now, but had known because of the operation that I would never be able to have. I am full of future plans. I know that Chase didn't want anymore children, but that was a couple years ago. He would certainly want this baby, it was created out of our renewed love for one another. We will make it right this time, make it work. We are both older now, wiser and mature. We know how much we mean to each other…what a blessing we will have.

Chase and I are sitting in his van when I tell him. He has a far away look in his eyes, and I think it is because he is in shock over the news. He asked me how this could be possible…I really don't have a clue "how"…but tell him what the Doctor has said…that it does happen, rarely, but it does. He says he has to go take care of something, and that he will talk to me later that night. He kisses me goodbye and I get out of the van in front of the apartments and go back to Cory's house.

It doesn't dawn on me when he doesn't call that night, I just think he got tied up with something and doesn't have the chance. It really doesn't dawn on me the next evening either, making up yet another excuse to myself when he doesn't call or come by. I start to wonder though by the third morning and call his Mother, Darla. She hasn't seen him either. She thought he was with me. She says she will make a few phone calls and see if she can locate him.

At 2 am the phone rings, I stumble for the phone thinking the worst has happened. It is Darla, she has found Chase, he is in Ohio, has moved back to his hometown…I was devastated. I was utterly destroyed.

I thought we were going to have a new beginning, thought he truly loved me and that we were going to make it work this time. I call Darla, I tell her I am pregnant, and that is why he ran. I go over to the motel that Darla manages and Sara is there, we sit in Darla's bedroom on her bed and talk about what has happened. I know in my heart it is hard enough to raise the two children I already have, but I can not have an abortion or give the baby up for adoption. I will keep it…my boy.

I am so sure in my mind that this is my little son, my new child. I dream about him..I tell him we will make it somehow. I even pick out his name, Chance. It is the perfect name for this baby, he is my chance at having my son. And, whether Chase likes it or not this baby will have the last name of Michaels.

I go back to the Doctor, he is upset at me for the weight I have lost, wants me to eat more. I tell him I am trying. My stomach stays upset partly due to the baby and because of the stress I am under. He tells me the baby is progressing well and gives me my due date…December 25th. Now I know that this will be my miracle baby.

You would think I would be used to the pitfalls in my life,

the constant hurt I seem to go through...but, I guess you never can get used to it. Just when I would think my life will be turning around, I get slapped down and then have to try to pick myself up again.

After all the concerns I had about this pregnancy, taking care of yet another child, yet wanting him so badly, even giving him his name...I wake up in the early morning hour to a pain in my stomach radiating around to my lower back., it is 4 am...My heart starts to race, I know what is happening to my body, I have felt the pain of labor before.

 I sit myself up as best I can in the bed, and feel a rush of fluids, the blood. I scream out for Cory and she comes running. She helps me to the bathroom, and into the shower helping me to clean up and put a pad on. The blood has slowed down to a trickle and I think maybe I won't lose the baby after all. I call the doctor, he instructs me to go to bed and stay there until I come into see him in a few hours. I do everything he instructs me to do..I lay there trying to be as still as I can and count the hours down, praying.

But, I can't stop thinking...wondering what I have done wrong this time that I am being punished yet again, Wondering if this was some kind of cruel trick being played on me. I feel another rush of blood and Cory helps me once again to the shower, I lose my baby...right there for my eyes to see. I pick up the tiny fetus and wrap him in a towel...the blood is down to a trickle again.

At 9 am I go to the doctor's and am immediately brought back to the office, my little fetus - my boy - in tow. He cleans me out and says it was a clean miscarriage, and gives me several prescriptions to take to start the healing process and return my uterus back to normal. He says the fetus is about 12 weeks gestation. I hear him say he is sorry...I don't care.. the tears begin to flow… bitter and angry at Chase, I go home and mourn the loss of my little baby, my son.

CHAPTER FIFTEEN

The children and I move in with my Father...the one man I hate. But I think that Cory has had to put up with me long enough, even though she says I can stay. I am at one of the lowest points in my life. I have no job, no car, no life. I feel like I am at the mercy of my Father once again. I go down and apply for Food Stamps and Welfare for the children. I have no feelings...I could care less if I live or die. My children are all I have and all I focus on. I go through the motions of getting them up and ready for school, cleaning house, cooking. Everything feels like its in slow motion, almost robotic. I feel useless that I can not find a job, raise my children with my own money...I begin to hate myself. I think I deserve everything that has happened to me.

Jennifer and Sara try to help me through this low point. Sara had just split with her husband, Derek, and so she is having a tough time as well trying to take care of her own little girl. I am caught somewhere between wanting to be a little girl again, and the woman I thought I once was becoming.

Living at home, my Father controls my movements, telling me when I can go and what time my curfew is. I am a grown woman with children of my own, and he is setting my curfew to be in the house by ten. I can't imagine that this is what my life is suppose to be like, but it is.

One afternoon I lose my temper against my Father. I am tired of being told what to do...tired of answering anything to a man that had abused me…and to some degree still is. Tired of being controlled by a man, this man, any man…when their only purpose in life is to hurt. I realize after the months of solitude that I am the only one that can change what has happened to me. I don't want to continue like this anymore.

My Father had an old blue Valiant car parked in the side yard he was trying to sell. I tell him that I will paint the inside and outside of his house for that old car if it runs. He agrees. I do the job in less than 5 days. I am pleased with myself for doing something, finally…on my own.

I go looking for a job, any job, and Sara tells me there is an opening at the Seafood Shop she works at. I apply, and I get it. Another accomplishment. I go off the food stamps and welfare….yet another accomplishment. Slowly I am gaining some of my self worth back.

Sara offers for me to come and live with her. It's a small apartment in town, with only one bedroom, but we can make do. I tell my Father I am moving out, and of course he is angry…and tells me Sara is just going to use me…we exchange harsh words, but I pack up and move out that very day.

Sara invites me to go out with her on the weekends, and at first I turn it down. I don't want to leave the children more than I have to. I don't trust anyone that lives with their father to baby sit, I don't want my children around any man without me being there. I am totally obsessed with the fact that what I have went through with my Father in my life, will never happen to my young girls. Finally she talks me into going, and even has her Mother babysit for me so that I won't worry.

I have the time of my life. The bar, the lights, the music….it is all so much fun. Sara and I laugh and dance and I even drink a little.

I begin to date I guy by the name of Rick Marlin. We have

fun together, go places together. We enjoy a good sexual relationship, but love for me is out of the question. We aren't together very long when he pops the question, asking me to marry him. I think, "No way. I am not ready for this." I don't want to lose this new freedom, it is to precious to me right now. I am just starting to grow, become my own woman. So the inevitable happens very quickly…we break up.

CHAPTER SIXTEEN

Now you want to meet a woman with a cool attitude, that was Sara. She was brought up to be mean and fiery, she is absolutely the strongest woman I have ever known. Most people think there is no way we could hit it off, me the introvert, and her truly the epitome of being the extrovert. But we did.

We complimented each other all the way down to the chores in the house. Sara showing me what life is outside my shell, things I had never seen and never thought of doing. I started to learn the powers a woman can have. Dressing up in my clothes, fixing my hair and make up just so, going out at night and dancing the night away with different men, or just each other if there was no one else.

She showed me what it was Chase had enjoyed so much about going to the bars: the fun and the freedom. I fixed my budget to be able to go out with her twice a month. It was outrageous. I loved the feeling, it was like a drug to me. And, drinking, well that allowed me to be someone else…and it felt good. I can forget the pain in my heart, the past, the loss of my Mother. All that I had is laughter and fun.

Sara and I decided to move into a two bedroom duplex we had found. It was not the grandest of places, but it did have French doors that led from the kitchen and living room to the front porch. It was our new home, with our own bedrooms which we would share with our children; we were so proud of it. We lived in the same house, worked at the same job and both came home smelling of fish every evening…It was a good life.

I loved this new found freedom I had. It was empowering to me that I could handle the bills on my own, dress how I wanted, juggle work and day care and feel the taste of freedom without someone's thumb being over my head.

But then Chase came back from Ohio. Some of the old patterns emerged, and we started seeing each other again. I am beginning to realize, that it seems that no-matter what Chase does, I seem to forgive him for it. I am drawn to him. He comes over out of the blue, stops by unannounced, we make love and he leaves again. He is like a drug I am addicted too, as long as the drug is away from me I am safe from its harm, but put it near me and I think I must have it. Only this time there is no "I Love You's". I do realize though, in growing up a little, that he has no idea what he wants out of life or from a woman. No one truly belongs to him, and he never belongs to anyone. He is constantly searching… searching.

Suddenly, he stops coming by, and I find out from friends he is dating another woman. I should be angry, search him out and cause a scene. I do nothing…it's just over.

I was so into this new side of me. I could go out all night if I wanted and sleep the next day if it was my day off. I could go and dance all night with men and then when the night was over, I could go home alone. I was laughing, joking, and for the biggest change of all…I was beginning to understand the word 'happy'.

I was smart about it though, I sheltered my children from seeing any of it. I would hire a babysitter that could keep them all night if I was going to be out drinking. They never saw me till the next morning when I had sobered up. I had enough intelligence to make sure my children were protected from any harm, even if that included me.

I was dating on a regular basis, new and exciting experiences. Sara being so bold and brash…how could I not have fun. Through her I would meet the most interesting people and do the most fascinating things. Not mommy things, Not kid things….regular 'I am free, watch me fly', kind of things.

I am sure I should have enjoyed as all of this as a teenager and young adult, to help me to grow into womanhood. But, my Womanhood had came way to early for me, there was no time to try new things, or be free…and learn what being bold and brash like Sara was all about.

I meet a man that totally blows me away. He is Derek's, Sara's ex-husband, best friend, and his name is Cal Richards. He asked Derek to set me up with him, and Derek had come over and told me about it. Asking if I would want to go out on a date with him…

This man, a man like I have never met before. Like a freight train coming at you at 100 miles an hour, you feel the fear and yet are excited by the rush of being in danger. He is a Harley-riding, black leather boots and vest kind of man. A pirate, a rogue.

He had long dark brown hair, and a long beard, and I was captivated by his 'bad boy' type of image. He is everything I have never been, and you could tell just by looking at him that he had seen and done it all. Fast moving and slow talking, shorter than any of the men I had ever dated, and 10 years older. I was in lust…no doubt about it. This relationship was based more on the silences then on the words. I could look into his eyes, and feel his heat. He boosted my ego, and made me feel for the first time in my life…sexy, alive and wanted. Not for the housewife I was, not for my dry humor, not because I was a good mother. But simply because I was me.

He took me to meet all his biker friends, to a life I had never understood and had barely been aware of before. He was way out of my league. But, I liked the feeling, it was new and dangerous to me. If my Father had hated Chase, he most definitely would not have liked Cal.

My Father was still calling, worrying me, stressing me out, but I was dealing with it. I darn sure wasn't going to bring Cal around for him to start on me about that., and Cal wasn't the type that I wanted my family to meet ... There was never a thought in my mind to take him home to meet the family.

Cal would sing songs to my girls before they went to bed, or tell them bed time stories. He kept that side of himself away from the outside world. He drank, he partied, and I am sure he did some drugs. Like I said he seemed dangerous, and I liked that about him. We would sit for hours and talk about nothing important. We would make love, and never utter a word. It was a strange relationship, but I liked it. He was independent, would come and go at will with no regular schedule to his life..

One afternoon he came in and told me he was moving back to Pennsylvania in two weeks and did I want to go with him. I told him my life was here, I didn't want to move my children to another state. He was cool with it, and we saw each other right up until two days before he moved. We said our goodbye's and when he walked out the door and fired the Harley up, I teared-up. But, it was done.

He did leave me with wonderful memories and had brought out a different woman in me, a passionate side I didn't know existed, one with a lot more confidence and awareness about my own body.

CHAPTER SEVENTEEN

I continued to work and do well at my job, earning raises after raises for all the hard work. I was proud of myself anytime I cashed my check, every time I took my children to McDonald's, or bought them something new.

Sara and I were the best of room mates, still having fun, still going out, still feeling the freedom of being single mother's with children. I could feel family around me anytime I went to visit her Mom, Cathy, or her Aunt Leslie and her daughter, Julia. We would go over to her Grandparent's house and have cook-outs…it felt like home. They were family., and I liked to watch this family with all it's love and affection, and they always made me feel welcome.

I was gaining a lot of new friends along the way, building my personality. I still saw Jennifer regularly, and saw Cory when I could get by to see her . It was the best time of my life. My friends had brought strength to my personality. It was as if the childhood memories that haunted me were being kept at bay. I wasn't having the nightmare's I had been so use to having through out my life. Life was getting easier, and I was growing even more as a woman.

A new guy comes into my life. He is hired as the new head Manager at the Seafood Store. Tall, Italian, and handsome, he was older than me by 11 years. He asked me out, and I excepted. His name was Mark Coccia, with dark hair, dark skin and deep dark eyes. He had come from the Detroit area when the plant he was working at closed down. His Mother lived in Florida, so he had packed up and came here till the plant reopened. He was seasoned, acted so mature and wise. We start to date. He tells me over and over how special I am. He would tell me I had witches eyes, said I could capture a man's heart when I looked at them.

I can not tell you honestly when or what happened, but, I think it was love. Whatever it was, I fell into it. If we were not working, we were together constantly, taking the children somewhere. I stopped going out with Sara and started focusing on Mark. He wanted me to be with him all the time…and I thought how special I was that a man wanted me that bad. If Sara did ask me to go somewhere and I excepted, he would get so gloomy and sad…that I would tell Sara I would have to cancel. He loved me so much, I couldn't say no to him.

We were dating for about six months when the call came in from Detroit that the plant was going back into production. The pay there was three times the amount he made here. He would be a fool not to go. He asked me to go, and to marry him. I thought about it for a little while, and said yes.

By now Chase was already married to his third wife, and I hadn't seen him in a long time. I don't know the reasons behind me wanting to go to Michigan when just a little over a year earlier I didn't want to go to Pennsylvania with Cal. But, I guess I had changed so much in that time that I was ready to love and be loved.

Sara was not happy about my decision, neither was Jennifer…they didn't want me to move so far away from them. Sara also had doubts about Mark, she liked him well enough and they got along great, but she just didn't think he was the right man for me. In the end, they both accepted whatever choices I decided to make.

Mark left ahead of us, he went back to work just two days after getting up there. He found a beautiful townhouse to live in, and sent me pictures of "our" new home. I couldn't believe how lucky I was. To have a man love me, truly love me. He called me every other night, he told me how much he missed me and couldn't wait for me to get up there.

The children and I set out on our own in my little car, bound for Detroit. Everything we could get of ours in the trunk of the car and above us on the roof in a carry-all. A whole new world was out there waiting for me. One week after we arrived, Mark and I got married. I was so happy, a nice place to live, two beautiful children and a new and exciting life to start.

The first time it happened I was absolutely stunned that I didn't even move. I was numb. A hit, hard to the face. We had been married almost two weeks. I had no idea what had provoked him, I still don't know what first started it. I did learn in the coming months that it could be something as simple as not fixing his dinner the right way. At first I fought back, but as the time went on, the fighting back got less and less.

He didn't want me to work, didn't want me associating with the neighbors - nothing. I was so bored at home during the day with the children both in school. I begged him to let me work, and finally one afternoon he said I could work if I found a part-time job. I did find a job, a little deli down the road from us…but I didn't get to keep it long. Mark would come up to my work and stand there watching me for the short hours I was there. It unnerved the Owner, Angelo. One afternoon, after repeatedly asking Mark to stop coming up there and getting shoved against the wall…I went in and told Angelo I had to quit. I didn't have to say much else to him…he already knew the answer.

CHAPTER EIGHTEEN

My oldest daughter, Sierra became ill and we had to rush her to the hospital. She is having convulsions and a high fever. The hospital can not get the fever down. Can not stop the convulsions…so they transfer her to the Children's Hospital outside Detroit. I call both mine and Chase's family members. Darla says she will be on the next plane out. Sierra is very sick and continues to convulse even with medications in her.

The doctors tell me they are not sure she will make it…they let me go to see her, she is in a fetal position and crying like a new born child…she is seven years old. Darla arrives at the airport and Mark greets her there and brings her to the hospital. We keep a vigil going for several days over Sierra. Mark treats me like a queen the whole time. They find that she has epilepsy, put her on the right medications, and like the trooper she is, she pulls out of it with flying colors. Darla goes home to Florida, and life with Mark returns to normal.

There are nights Mark doesn't come home and I am glad when he doesn't…it means that my night will be free from the hitting. I finally get up the courage to ask him why he even married me if he was going to be so cruel…his answer hurt me much more than anything he had yet to say to me, and to this day…I still remember it: "I married you to take care of my house, why else would a man marry a woman with kids?"

Sara comes up for two weeks to see me, and as usual Mark's performance is excellent., he is on his best behavior. Sara and

I have a wonderful time, Mark takes us out to dinner several times…We are acting like the married couple. I don't tell Sara anything and have hidden my bruises well underneath my make-up..I am used to hiding them.

I hated to see her leave, I knew what would happen after she was gone. But, still I could not bring myself to tell her anything, even though I could have when he was at work. I knew if I told her, she would lash out at him and then when she left to go back to Florida, I would get it from him three times as hard.

One might say " Why didn't you leave him,"and my answer would have been."why?" From the first hit, from the first time he forgot to come home…I believed somehow I deserved it…one major hit, it's all it takes and everything you have tried to learn and tried to repair about your damaged life, goes right down the trash. I was just the same scared little girl I was under my Father's watchful eye…still being controlled and disciplined. This was a huge pattern in my life…child abuse, verbal abuse, sexual abuse…it is all the same. The same kind of fears and feelings of worthlessness….

My Father calls from Florida with a huge job proposal for Mark. One that he accepts before ever getting off the phone or even telling me about it. He tells me he is taking a leave of absence from his job and we are moving back to Florida. He is going to head my Father's trucking company. I have no idea what on earth he is talking about, last I had heard my Father had one truck. I don't argue about it, I knew better than to speak my opinion. I was just happy to be going back to Florida…Where my friends were, where I would be safer.

We move in with my Father, I absolutely hate the idea...but I know that I will not get hit there and it is just long enough to find a place to live.

Mark finds out as soon as we arrive that the Trucking

company was all a hoax to get us to move back. Mark is extremely angry and I think there will be a fight. I think I am going to be in a lot of trouble when Mark gets me alone. Instead he slams out of the door and leaves the yard. My Father tells me why he pulled off the bogus job offer, he says he found out I was being beat. So, he found a way to get me back home. I know of only two people that could have told him anything, Darla or Sara…but neither one had seen anything.

I do finally find out that Sara was the one that called my Father when she had got back home. Though she didn't have the proof, she could feel something wasn't right. It was the first time I would credit my father for getting involved in my life.

Mark and I then move into a house across from Jennifer. Mark try's to make it appear that we are a normal married couple. There is nothing normal about it though, and Jennifer knows it immediately. Mark goes back to his old ways, hitting me…Jennifer comes by more often unannounced. She keeps check on me…unnerving Mark.

One afternoon, while I am at work at the nearby 7-11, Jennifer calls. Mark is packing up everything he owns in his car. I can not leave the store, there is no one to cover for me as I am the only one there. By the time I can get off work and rush home, his car is gone, all of his stuff and some of my stuff are missing from the house. There is no note. I go to the bank to check on the money in our checking account. He has taken it all…the rent, the electric, even the grocery money…all gone. Another marriage down the tubes in less than a year. I am in financial trouble, but I make a solemn promise to myself…I will never get hurt like this again.

I leave my job at the 7-11 for a better paying job as a receptionist. It is more money than I have ever been used to making. That at least starts to make me feel good again...

Chase separates from his third wife soon after this...and of course he and I start seeing each other again for a short period of time. I haven't even taken the time to try and get over this last blunder of a marriage before I jump into the fire with Chase...No time to get over the abuse I have just went through. We move into a two bedroom duplex together down the street from his Mother, and decide to split the bills 50-50. This time we are not just seeing each other from time to time, we are living together.

Unfortunately, it doesn't last long. His old patterns emerge and I try to hold on by watching his every move and demanding more attention than he can give. One afternoon the phone rings and there is a woman on the other end...she ask who I am and I tell her my name, "ohh, his ex-wife"she says. I reply "yes". "Well then maybe you are the one I want to talk to," and I say "ok."

She tells me point blank.."I am pregnant with Chase's child"...and she hangs up on me.

I ask Chase about it when he comes home, I demand to know who this witch is. He says he has no idea what I am talking about. The argument gets heated, and before I realize it I am in the bedroom, slumped on the floor, crying hysterically. I had finally lost it, I guess. I was tired of all the disappointments. He could go, just get the hell out...go live his life . Chase packs up his belongings and leaves...

CHAPTER NINETEEN

I am absolutely bewildered about my life. My world had fallen apart so many times, and I have tried to pick the pieces up and to drown the pain deep down within me. I have tried to be strong where there is no strength, and yet here I am again trying to pick the pieces up yet again and try to repair the damage.

My Father starts his "I told you so'", coming around and calling me, getting on my last nerve. Telling me I can't handle life, telling me I get taken advantage of because I don't listen to him. There are times when he acts like he wants to start a "fresh" relationship…but there is no way I can get close to him. He is dating a woman he plans to marry…and I know he is hoping that if he gets on my good side, I will not tell her the dirty secret about the past. I don't buy into it. I just want him to go live his life and let me live mine.

But, for my brother and sister…I at least endure him at the Thanksgivings, Christmas's and family reunions to be with them.

I get a big promotion at work and move up from Receptionist to Accounts Receivable. I am living on my own in the duplex with my daughters and paying all the bills on my own. Slowly over the next several months I start to get some of my self-reliance back. I take the children out every Friday night, and do the things I want to do without being told what is right or wrong, or what I can or can not do. I get very good at managing my money. I take another part-time job cleaning houses.

I need no one for anything. I don't go out without the children, I don't date. I am so bitter toward men that I have decided that I don't want anything more to do with them.

I had come to the end of my rope, starting with my Father and ending yet again with Chase. There were no such things as the fantasy becoming reality. No rainbow with the gold on the other end....all of it a ruse someone painted to make life seem more enjoyable.

Friends of mine try to get me to go out, try to set me up with dates...they hate to see me alone. I decline all their offers. The men at work ask me out, I decline them also. I tell them all… "I do not date."

Several of Chase's friends come by and ask me out, again I say no. No dates, and No man…its exactly what I mean. There will be no reason to be hit by a man, no excuses for being told they love me one minute, just to walk out the door the next. No reason to answer to anyone. I can come and go as I please, and make myself a solemn promise to myself, "I will never allow myself to be hurt again". I build the walls tall and thick around me…and I plan on them staying that way..

I move up in the Company I work for, not only am I handling Accounts Receivable, but now I am handling Payroll and the Irrigation division of the company I work for. I am working Monday through Friday in this job, then working Saturday afternoon's cleaning houses, and cutting hair on Saturdays or Sundays.

I become the head of the Irrigation division, Hiring, firing and scheduling jobs. My life is full. The girls and I have every evening together and watch television till it is time for bed. Every Friday night like clock work, we go out to eat and see a movie. I like this way of life….

A lot can change in 12 month's though…can't it?

This man starts to work for our company, in fact I am his boss. His name is Ian Hollis, a tall hugely built man with deep dark skin and dark brown hair. He tries on many occasions to flirt with me, but I don't notice and certainly don't respond. I had become the blunt of jokes at my job, dominated mostly by men, for some time now. I had been asked out and had turned down every man that was single that worked there, so the men started calling me "Ice Princess." With every new guy that started there, the other men would warn them: "You can't get a date with the Ice Princess…there's just no way." Well that must have been a challenge to this new guy, Ian, because every chance he got he was trying to talk to me.

I did not like him that was for sure. He had these huge muscles underneath his short sleeved T-Shirts. I never liked men with big muscles. He was loud, boisterous, a comedian…he walked too tall , acted to proud, and was too darn sure of himself. He spoke his mind and was way to honest for my liking.

He winked at me to much, called me darling in front of the other men, and he just unnerved me…I just didn't care for him or his type; a biker/cowboy looking renegade…with a deep southern drawl.

He heard that I cut hair on the side, so he comes up to me one afternoon and asks if I will cut his hair. What the heck I need the money. I can get his hair cut and have him out of my house in 15 minutes.

He came on a Saturday afternoon and I cut his hair, he paid me and I started showing him to the door… "Couldn't he stay for a glass of tea" he asked me, smiling with his eyes. I was stuck, didn't know how to usher him out any quicker than by opening the door and hoping he would get the hint. I told him he could, but told him it had to be a quick glass and then he would have to go.

A week goes by, my radiator goes out on my car as I am going to work. I figure I can nurse it along until I get the money saved up. I really wasn't worried about it. The mechanic at our shop helps me out by filling it with water before I leave each evening from work. I fill it each morning as I head to work. It will get me by.

I hear a noise outside of my house and look out the window to find Ian is putting in a new Radiator. I open the door quickly and yell to him.."What do you think your doing?" demanding an answer "Take that back out of there!" We argue back and forth about it with both of us finally winning. He puts the radiator in, and I will pay him so much per week till it is paid off. I turn and shut the door and leave him out there with his tools and the radiator.

For three months this goes on, back and forth. He would bring pizza over and bribe my girls with it till I would let him in. He would bring stuffed animals he had bought somewhere and hand them to me as I opened the door, I would then hand them to the kids. He would stop by with groceries, enough for three days worth, and ask me if he could stay for dinner, and I would tell him I didn't want nor need his generosity…

Finally I give in and go out on a date with him, with my children. I figure he would leave me alone after that - he didn't. I even had him babysit the children for me for six hours while I went off with a friend of mine. I thought that he would be tired by the time I got home of two rambunctious children bugging him all day for things to do. Oh no..I came home to find that he had taken them out to McDonald's for lunch, .then came back and cleaned up the house, done my laundry, fed the children, got them ready for bed, and my dinner still hot in the oven. That plan hadn't worked.

84

One night he tells me that he kept pursuing me because of what I had said to him with my eyes. He said he was watching me work, and he heard a little girls voice say "I'm suffering, I'm not happy, help me." From that moment on he was hell bent on being with me, and at every turn he was. It didn't matter the hour. He was beginning to act like more like a stalker, yet I wasn't afraid of him in that way. Every wall he tried to knock down around me..I would hurry and build up another.

He told me he loved me, and I would ask him to leave. He would ask me out on other dates, I would say no. But, one night while he was sitting across the room watching t.v., as if he belonged there, he asked me "Can I kiss you?"...and my answer to him was "I don't know, can you?"

We made love for the first time a week or so after that. It had been well over a year and a half since I had been with a man. I was extremely nervous. I didn't have the feeling like I had so many times before, that if we made love, he owned me or I belonged to him. No, this was more about sexual satisfaction. He took his time with me, as if he knew it had been a long time, he experienced me in ways I had never imagined. He knew it too, knew he was able to push the right buttons to make me come alive in bed. I enjoyed him, and it helped that he was excellent in bed.

But as soon as we were done, I would tell him to leave, and he would.. I couldn't stand the thought of him being in my house over night, not in my bed...not anywhere. I sent him home time after time again...

One night after making love I told him once again that he had to leave...only this time he balked at it, and told me if he walked out the door this time, he wasn't coming back...I told him to go ahead and leave, I didn't care...only I didn't expect that when he slammed the door behind him, my heart would fall to the floor.

CHAPTER TWENTY

Ian had told me for months that he loved me. I had ignored him at every turn…now it looked like the one thing I tried to avoid happening did: I was becoming attached to this strange man. I was stubborn though and left him alone. No matter how much I wanted to talk to him, no matter how much I wanted to see him…I acted as though it didn't matter. It was so hard to pull off since we both worked at the same place. But I held my ground and didn't let him know what I was feeling.

I found myself missing the conversations we had, he could keep up with me on politics' and religion…we could debate all kinds of subjects.

I found myself missing his masculine smell, the feel of his large arms on me when we were in bed. The softness to his hair and the hardness of his skin against mine. I would catch myself looking at him when he wasn't looking. I would watch his muscles under his shirt as he worked. I would study his face as he talked to the other workers, careful for him not to see me. It hadn't dawned on me how handsome he was…his dark toned skin and those large green looking eyes.

One afternoon, he came by my house and as usual, expectantly I opened the door, and he asked if we could talk…I was so glad to see him there, I just threw my arms around him, darn me anyway. I think that both of us were shocked at my actions.

The next time he came by to see me he had his clothes with him and as he walked into the house, said he was moving in with me. I argued the point, rather verbally. I wasn't ready for any commitments just yet. It was all too soon. I wasn't ready to have a man walk in and take over my life again when I had tried so hard to gain my independence, and my own self confidence. He asked me to give him a chance, if it didn't work out within the next three months, he would leave and never bother me again. But, if it did work, and if I told him I loved him, then at the end of the three months he would ask me to marry him. After much arguing, I agree to his terms.

My father finds out that Ian and I are together, and starts calling me about how I am messing my life up again. He tells me Ian is into drugs and is a drunk...anything to upset me. I try to explain to him that I know about Ian's past...that he is clean and sober now...and that's all that matters, but He won't leave it be.

One afternoon, while on the phone yet again with my Father, trying to explain myself, listening to him ridicule me...Ian says he has to go somewhere and will be back as soon as he can. What I didn't know was that Ian went over to my Father's house, and told him, no... demanded, for him to leave me alone and stop calling and harassing me. He tells my Father he is tired of him constantly putting me under pressure, constantly upsetting me and that if it doesn't stop...he will come back and hurt him. My Father acts like he is going for his knife that is in his pocket...but Ian doesn't back down....He tells him this is the last time, he won't threaten me nor will he threaten him anymore...and that by the time he got to his "pig sticker" he would snap his neck. The calls from my Father end.

Ian and I touch on many subjects that I had never shared with anyone else. I tell him some of the things in my past. I am honest with him about Chase and the fact that I still love him no matter what he has done in the past. Ian tells me he feels the same way about his ex-wife, Elaine. He tells me he understands the power of a first love, especially when they are the parent of your children.

I am floored...he doesn't want to change me? Make me hate this ex- spouse.. he says he would never exclude Chase from my life or that of my children's life.

We are about four months into the relationship when a baby comes into the picture. His second wife, ex-wife, has had a baby and the friend that calls him tells him that his name is on the birth certificate. When she had left him, she had told him the baby wasn't his, he assumed it to be true until now, seven months later. We find the child, a girl... We also find out she is being put up for adoption. His ex-wife, Mary, has told the authorities that the baby's father is dead. Ian ask me to help him fight for his child, his first daughter with Elaine has always been kept away from him except for once- and- awhile visits....he doesn't want to go through life with losing yet another child.

I think long and hard about it, I ask Sierra and Hannah what they think about it...we all agree to help him get his baby, and I will help raise it. Ian and I make a vow, that if we get the baby, neither of us can leave each other till the baby is old enough to leave the nest.

We won't put this child through what our children have went through in life by not being in a two parent family.

We let the lawyer we hire fight for us, but there really is no battle. Ian is very much alive and since the Mother was putting the child up for adoption, he is granted sole custody of the baby, a little girl...her name is Angela. I now have a third child, and she will fill the void I still feel for the child I lost years ago...

I become very sick and Ian stays by my side all the time now. I bleed for seven months non-stop. I go in over and over for D&C's to be done, but they don't work, the bleeding returns. We go through six doctors trying to find out what is wrong. I take different medications with each doctor and each doctor is certain that the new medications will work.

Each D&C doesn't show any oddities within it. I am losing strength, I try to remain strong and determined and go to work even though I now have to wear baby diapers to catch the flow of blood. There are trips to the Hospital when I hemorrhage, new doctors that try the same tired things only for nothing to change.

Ian has to fix a pot of coffee and bring it to me... I have to drink the full pot to get enough strength to get out of bed. He has to help me dress for work.

All the fears I have had for so long about my body being shown in the light of day, go out the window. Ian sees it all. Many nights he wakes me, carries me to the shower and to bathe the blood off of me, then changes the bedding because I had bled all over myself, the bed and him…

Ian finds the seventh doctor himself and sets up the appointment. He finds that he is a highly reputable man. We have all my medical files sent over from the other six doctors offices.

I go into this office, he already has my file before him at his desk….without even checking me internally he tells me he knows what is wrong but can't prove it until he removes my uterus…the lining of my uterus, that all the other doctor's had focused on was not the fault. The uterus itself, the muscle itself, is cancerous. I must have a surgery, a hysterectomy, immediately.

I tell Ian the findings from the doctor, and my fears of not being a woman anymore after the operation. I read to him reports about some women that have no more sexual feeling after a radical hysterectomy. I am so afraid I will be one of them. He tells me not to worry. He doesn't want to lose me…no matter what. He has stood by my side through out the whole ordeal, no matter how ugly it got. We will also get through this together.

CHAPTER TWENTY ONE

I go in for the surgery, as the doctor is afraid to wait any longer because my body is so weak. The surgery itself goes well, and they remove everything except one ovary, but I had complication's while in surgery. The doctor comes out and speaks to Ian; who is frantic because the surgery has taken much longer than the doctor said it would. The doctor relates to Ian that I stopped breathing while on the operating table, my blood pressure had dropped dangerously low and they had to resuscitate me. They believed it was the combination of the anesthesia they had given me and the fact that my body was so weak from so much blood loss...

When I woke up in the hospital bed, there was Ian...he had been there all night, sitting and sleeping in a chair next to me. I am on morphine the first few days and have hallucinations. He sits and listens to me ramble on. He stays with me every night until I am released.

He takes a short leave of absence from work to be home and take care of me when I get out of the hospital, waiting on me hand and foot. He cares for the children, cleans the house, does the cooking and the laundry.

He has not abandoned me through this whole ordeal..and I am grateful to him for rising to the occasion.

Ian asks me repeatedly to marry him through the next couple of years, and each time he asked I tell him I'm not ready yet. To me it is safer to live together, if something does go wrong we can still just get out of the relationship, with no divorces to deal with.

We have been together a little over three years when he comes home from work one morning and says, "Get dressed, we are going to go get married.". I argued the point with him, again trying to tell him I am not ready to commit. But, this time, he doesn't take it lightly- " If you don't go with me to get married today..then the relationship is over...if you aren't ready by now to marry me, you never will be..." he argues back

I decide finally just to throw caution to the wind and do it…we take Angela over to our friend's that lives nearby, Troy and Lisa's house. Lisa says she will watch after the baby while we go to get married. At ten in the morning we are married, by noon he was back to work.

Ian and I start a business together, and work long and hard alongside each other, raising calves from birth and selling them when they get to three months of age. We did this in the evenings while he still works his regular job and I take care of the house and children during the day.

Out of nowhere we were hit with a new stress to deal with. Suddenly the tables turn on us and Ian becomes ill.

It first started as just a right leg that swelled and no matter how much he tried to rest it or elevate it, it just would not stop swelling. Finally I talked this workaholic man into going to the doctor. He was put in the hospital immediately, spending two weeks there. He had blood clots in his legs and in his lungs.

For the next two years and over 15 trips to the hospital our world turned upside down. Several times the doctors said they doubted he would make it through the night, but he would. His medical history, and the new illnesses that kept happening to him seemed like something out of a Steven King novel than our real life.

The doctor's disabled him from ever working again, which only brought on a whole new set of problems. He was a man's man. He had been brought up to work hard, and had done so most of his life since he had been raised on a ranch. Now the doctor's were telling him he would never work again. The good man that I had come to know..was now infuriated, angry at himself for not being able to care for his family properly...so here we were again...another monkey on both of our backs.

We had learn to deal with it and all the frustrations and interruptions of constant visits to the doctors, which by this time consisted of eight. There was hospital stays, the worry and the wonder of what would be happening next..

One afternoon he made the decision that he would decide how he would live and it would be no where near the "lay down and die approach," the doctor's had asked of him. Instead he would get up everyday, no matter how badly he was feeling, do things the doctor's had asked him not to do, walk on his legs longer than he should.

He was learning strength against adversity...we both were. We made the best of the situation. There was no time for "poor me attitudes"..we would handle this the best way we could. I would go to work full time outside the home and we sell all the stock we had incurred in our young business, and just learn to get by in a different way.

The role was now reversed with me working as many hours as I could get in and Ian at home, doing what he could to help take care of the now teenager girls and our two- year- old daughter. The two oldest helped me with taking care of the house and laundry on the days I could not be home to do it. It is a tough adjustment all of us as a family have to learn to cope with.

CHAPTER TWENTY TWO

My Father passes away. I have very few tears...nothing like a child should have for the passing of a parent. Certainly nothing like the tears shed when my Mother passed away.

I tell myself he is gone now, he will never control me again. I am safe from him for the rest of my life. He won't come into my dreams anymore, won't disrupt my life with the bad memories I can't ever seem to shake. I know that the turn of events will make me stronger, wiser and I will deal with life so much better now....

Several months go by and my sister Gale stops by to see me as she usually had done...but for some reason on this day we start reminiscing about the past. In a long conversation about our Mom, she tells me that she felt so much pain because of her being so young (14) and finding our Mother's body on that fateful night.

I say to her ..."What are you talking about...that can't be....the police report said that Father found her when the two of you returned from Church that night."

I start to repeat myself as she is shaking her head "NO!..."

"But Gale" I start to say....she cuts me off and tells me her side of the story: "Dad didn't go to Church that night, he dropped me off and then left...and he didn't find Mom either.. he sent me into the house and told me to go find out if Mom was alright.. so I went to her bedroom and I found her...."

I told her once again what the police report said...Then I

went in search of it and showed her what our Father had told the police.

He had stated, right there in black and white...to the detective...that "He went to church with his daughter, and when he returned the house was dark ... he went inside and went to the bedroom, opened the door and something kept the door from opening all the way so he turned on the light and found her...he then knelt down next to her, picked up the gun, realized what he had done and dropped it back down..."

Gale repeats yet again that is not what happened...

My mind wonders back to when Chase had insisted all those years ago that my Mom did not commit suicide...that my Father might have done it. "Could what Chase have said been true? and if he didn't do it, then why would my Father lie to the Detectives about his alibi?"

Even more than that ..."Could it answer the question no one had the answer for...how did Mom know what to do with a gun since she had never held one let alone use one?"

I show the evidence to Ian..I ask him to form his own opinion. He does think it is a little fishy, but says ..."Your Father is dead...how will anyone ever know for sure"?

"I guess no one,"I say.

But then my mind would not stop thinking about it...I still need the answers. I need to know if my Mother committed suicide, leaving us to feel the pain we have dealt with all of these years or was her life taken, so that she could not be there to love us....I just have to know.

I call the Police department, and ask for the Sergeant that worked the case; the one listed on the report still works there. They said he does, but is not in...and they will have him call me.

Within a few hours of my call, Sergeant James calls me back.

I refer him to the case number and ask him if he would find it for me and then call me back. He says he will. He does. I repeat to him what the police report says, and he agrees with what I am saying as he has the same report sitting in front of him on his end of the phone. I then tell him what my sister has told me. Nervously I ask him, "Were prints ever retrieved from the gun?"

He stated, "Now, we didn't retrieve any because everyone had an alibi for the night she died, and with a past history of suicide attempts, we clearly thought it was suicide." I then asked his opinion about what I had told him my sister said had taken place. And his answer was: "If we had known your Father didn't have an alibi and there had been a window of a half hour or more that he could not have explained…with the evidence that his finger prints would have been on the gun because he clearly stated in the report he had picked it up and put it back down…then.. no.. we would have not treated it like a suicide."

My heart sinks…the Sergeant tells me I can reopen the case…and even though my Father is dead…we can clear it up on the files if I want to. It is more than I can handle at the moment and tell him "No, not right now." The thought alone is hard to swallow…I can not handle any other stress right now.

Several months have gone by since I had talked with the Sergeant regarding our Mother's case.. As with all the other times in my life I can not tell my brother, Jack, anything about what I have found out. He would never believe me, would call me a liar. He still holds his Father on a pedestal, so he would never believe my Father would have ever done anything wrong.

We get word from Chase's sister that he has been in a terrible motorcycle accident and may not live. I call his brother, Derek, at the hospital and he tells me everything he knows, and how serious this all is. "His face is split wide open," Derek relays to

97

me, "He has burns from the road and pieces of imbedded gravel deep in his skin." Chase was on a motorcycle run and drinking heavily...he had skidded over 500 feet across the road's pavement. It is the first time I am thankful for his drinking. If he had been sober his body would not have been as limber through the accident and he would have been dead at the scene. I was so grateful when I walked into his room and saw that even though he was in a great deal of pain, he will live and with surgery his face will be almost normal.

Six months later, my middle daughter, Hannah, yells out that her Dad is outside. We all walk out there to see him. This is not a normal visit by far...he has come to apologize to the children for not being there while they were growing up, he apologizes to me for the drinking that ruined our marriage. He tells me he is very proud of me for being a good Mom....He thanks Ian for raising the children as if they were his own. He makes a promise to both girls that he will spend the rest of his life making it all up to them. This is a new man we see standing before us. He has a new wife, children, and a new lease on life. I am very proud of him for the strength and the courage it took to come and talk to us about this.

My oldest daughter gets married and starts a family of her own. She moves 30 miles away, but she is happy and healthy and we see her often. It is a huge transition for me to lose one of my children from the nest, but I think I am dealing with it quite well. My second daughter is doing well and dating....Ian's two daughters are doing well, though we don't get to see them as often as we would like. And our daughter, the youngest, is in school and growing up before our eyes, too quickly.

Soon after Sierra's marriage she becomes pregnant, and we wait impatiently for our first grandchild to be born.

Ian's health is at its worse and we all fear he will not make it till the birth . He has been taking a drug called Interferon Alpha 2B, his liver is deteriorating, and this new drug is supposed to, in most cases, regenerate it. But he is not responding, so we fear the worse will happen. He has finally been diagnosed with all that is wrong with him. He has Mixed Connective Tissue Disease, an illness similar to lupus, a blood clotting disorder known as Anti-phospholipid Syndrome, liver disease, and diabetes. The Doctor's have given him five years to live.

We pray constantly that he will hang on long enough to see this child, our granddaughter Leesa, born. Amazingly, he does…and the sound of Leesa's brand new cry does something miraculous to Ian. Even though the doctor's take him off the medication because he is not responding, his liver does not deteriorate any further. To this day he believes that Leesa, who he affectionately calls his "Angel Baby" gave him the will to live.

We have learned to deal with all that has happened to Ian regarding his health, and have learned to cope with the hardships in our lives. With so many impossible challenges looming over us for so long, we are proud of the fact that we have risen above it, dodged it as best we could and have learned to cope.

CHAPTER TWENTY THREE

It seems like it was over night, though I know it wasn't. My sweet, second oldest daughter starts to change. The new boyfriend in her life seems to monopolize all of her time. She starts talking back, getting angry more often than she ever had in her life. Hannah had always been the easy child, easy going…suddenly it was as if she was brain washed and ashamed of us. Spending most of the holidays through out the year with her boyfriend's family. It only gets much worse when they became engaged.

My oldest daughter Sierra had planned a surprise Mother's day brunch at a very posh restaurant on the water way about 40 miles from us. Hannah was part of the plan until the night before when she announces to Sierra that she won't be going, she is spending Mother's Day with her soon to be Mother-in -Law. Sierra is angered by it but tries to keep it from me. I know something is up though when Hannah leaves early that morning and then all the girls, My other daughters, Ian's Mother and myself all get in the car. I question Sierra about it and she finally tells me….

That evening, Hannah comes in and I make mention of her spending the entire day with his family and not with me. I was hurt by her actions. Instead of explaining, she yells that she is moving out. I get angry, probably angrier than I should have, but I tell her "If she is going to move out, don't take just a few things…take it all." Hannah calls her boyfriend and together

they move all her things...my heart is torn apart.
If our lives were not complicated enough... I become ill. It
starts out like the flu. Only I could not seem to shake it. I
constantly have a headache, and at times I don't have any energy.
There is dizzy spells, vomiting, fevers....and all the doctor's
keep saying over and over is it's just the flu.
I lose all reflexes on my right side, have trouble walking
and using my arm. Ian goes back with me to the doctor...and
demands they run more tests. He does a series of blood tests
and then finally an MRI to the brain because of the headaches...I
can not walk without Ian walking on the right side to keep me
from falling over.
The Doctor calls in the evening the next day , and says to
me "I want you to go to a neurologist in St. Pete." I want to
know why and he says, "The MRI shows an aneurysm in your
brain...I want you to go see this Doctor day after tomorrow he
will be able to explain it better."
I tell Ian what the Doctor has just said, we both just sit there
numb...this can't be happening.
Ian and I take the films with me to the neurologist....who
tells me not only did I have an aneurysm in the cerebral cortex
but I have a lesion in the occipital lobe as well and that I have
had a Stroke. I am put on medication immediately and sent to a
Physical Therapist to help me to regain some of the strength
back in my right side. I would have to walk with a cane and
have someone help me till I gained the strength back... the
aneurysm is in-operable..it is too far in the cerebral cortex.
If that wasn't enough to swallow, my primary doctor calls
me back two days after seeing the neurologist with the blood
test results. I have a positive Epstein-Barr and
Cystomegalovirus, the diagnosis: Chronic Fatigue Syndrome,
an autoimmune disorder that causes the fatigue and flu-like

symptoms I had been experiencing for so long. The pain I have been feeling in my muscles he diagnosis as Fibromyalgia, a piggy-back disorder of Chronic Fatigue Syndrome.

I give up on the Physical Therapist, I want to get better faster than they are helping me to do. I refuse to go outside and be seen walking with a cane. Night after night Ian sits by me on the couch as I raise and lower a small child's rocker first, and then after several weeks, I start lifting his leg up and down, night after night we would do this while watching TV, with me holding a tennis ball in my right hand and squeeze it over and over until the strength in my right arm and hand returns .

If Ian becoming sick hadn't been enough, if our lives hadn't been changed due to losing his income, now that I was sick it was even worse… making our lives even more stressful than they already were.

I can not tell you what exactly happened shortly after that time but, I know it did happen. I woke up one morning with no will to go on…I was absolutely suicidal. I didn't want to get out of bed, I didn't want to eat…all I wanted was to be left alone to sleep. Ian didn't understand, knew something was wrong, tried to think of a quick fix…to no avail. I couldn't tell him what was happening…all I felt was doom.

My mind would play tricks on me. I would remember conversations between my Father and I that had been put to rest long before he died. I started recalling the past sexual abuse, and would lay there and cry and beg myself to stop allowing this. If I didn't have weird day dream, then I would wake up at night with awful nightmare's…

Every detail that had happened would flood into my mind like it was yesterday…and along with it I felt the pain of it all over again. My unborn baby came into my mind, that I needed to hold him just once. I would have visions of a tiny baby crying out and I couldn't find him...my ears would fill with the sounds. The memories of what Rick had done came screaming into my mind, as if it had just happened. All the memories were occurring in my mind, not one by one...but all at once like a flash of pictures before your eyes at rapid speed. There was no separation of the years, it was all coming into mind at one time, haunting me, tearing me apart. I was losing control and didn't even realize it.

Ian tried to call a Doctor, wanted me to go to the hospital...but I threatened him that if he did I would kill myself before they could take me away. No one was taking me away. In my mind, I wasn't going to be sent somewhere like my Mother was...I wouldn't go through the electric shock treatments she had endured. Yet, he knew I was on the edge, hanging by a thread and saying things that didn't make sense....crying uncontrollably.

Ian sat by my bed for days on end, willing me to live...holding my hand, wiping the tears away...taking me to the bathroom...making me eat something.

All the things that had happened to me from the time I was a little girl, things I had buried deep down inside me and tried to overcome were all back now, full force and trying to destroy me.

I was the star in a bad horror flick and the demons were circling me....days were spent in bed, days of uncontrollable crying.

Ian would just sit in a chair next to my bed and patiently wait for me to talk. I would choke on the words when I spoke, trying desperately to get out the pain and frustrations...I would scream at Ian in between the sobs and try to tell him how I felt about my Father...how could a Father do something so cruel to his own child, he was so sick and perverted, he didn't deserve to have a family.

He needed to apologize to me for what he put me through...
"Damn him, the son-of-a-bitch. I hate him"...and I told Ian all
the sick things he did to me, every nasty sordid detail of my
childhood. Ian cried as the words come flowing out.

The constant threats. He is the one that started all of this. He
made me feel worthless, ugly, and stupid. He is the one that
kept me from being strong and fighting for what I believed in.
He had abused me, hurt me more than anything in life ever
could...he was the reason the Nightmares Echoed.....

My Father had chastised me for my choice of men, my
marriages and divorces. But, wasn't he the one that helped to
create this lack of security that I had felt most of my life? Wasn't
he the one that set me up to fail at everything I did? The more
that the days changed into night, the angrier I became and the
more I reached out to Ian and spoke about my feelings.

I was going to get better, I had to get better... I did have
courage and perseverance, I had to have, I just didn't realize it
till I fell apart...To go through everything I did as a child
including the surgeries, I had to have had courage and
determination...

I asked myself.. "Where was this little girl's family...why
couldn't they see what my Father was doing....why couldn't
they look past his lies and see the real child that I was? Why
didn't it dawn on them when I ran away from home, and wasn't
with Chase...that something was terribly wrong." Why did what
my Father say mean more to family members than what I had
to say.

Why was my Mother dead...when she had been far superior
to my Father? Why couldn't he have died for the sins he had
done in his life, leave her living for us to love and be with; so
many questions...WHY?

The guilt also began to surface. I hated myself for being so weak that I had allowed Rick or Mark into doing the things they had done. Oh, yes I hadn't been a good wife to Rick, and yes, I should never have married someone I didn't love...but damn him...he was at fault too. He had preyed on me knowing I was vulnerable from losing Chase. He knew how much Chase had meant to me. Was marrying me his way of one- upping Chase? Did he laugh inside when we had gotten married...after all he had gotten Chases's ex-wife. I had been no more than a joke.

Then Mark, who did he think he was....I had truly cared for him, I wanted a life with him. I gave up everything in Florida to move to Michigan to be with him. He had lied about loving me. I had not deserved to be hit by him. He was selfish and inconsiderate of anyone but himself and took his own insecurities out on me.

Chase was next. He had been the man of my dreams, the man I had admired in my screwed up world. He had saved me from so much hurt, the man that had rescued the damsel in distress. But he had abandoned me when I needed him most. He replaced drinking for his family. How could a boss, any boss, ever be more important than that....I know I was screwed up with some of my ways....too over-protective, to clingy. But, why couldn't he help to fight, find a way to deal with it? It became to easy to walk away, when I needed him most.

When he came back into my life again, why didn't he tell me up front that I was just something to have while in between relationships. It had been so easy to walk away again, knowing I was pregnant with his baby. He couldn't trust me, the only person on earth that he could have ever trusted.

I lost my baby because of him; and then he went on to have babies later on with another woman. Didn't I deserve my baby too? Didn't I deserve to have more children?

The anger was releasing from my body, I could feel it lifting like a huge weight off of my shoulders. I finally, silently, was telling each and every person that had hurt me what I was feeling. They may not have heard it....but I knew it within myself....The Demons that thought my soul was home to them were being cast away one by one.

CHAPTER TWENTY FOUR

I slip out of my bed and walk over to the mirror on the dresser. I look at myself, probably for the first time in my life I really look. I look at my face, side views than the front. I look closer...deeper. For years I have only looked at what my Father saw..a homely, ugly girl.

I remember the things that Chase had told me when I was young. I was pretty, and that I was sexy. Cal had told me the same things when I was a little older, adding that I had beautiful eyes, cat- like, devilish, and witch-like. Ian has been telling me for years that I am pretty, a pretty face, beautiful breasts, and a great rear-end. I have never seen it in all of my life the things that they have seen. I always laughed off what they had said, always thinking it was their way of being nice to me...giving me compliments to make me feel good about myself.

This day though, I am really going to look..look past what I have seen for years and really study what these men have seen. I am going to try and look from their point of views and not what I have been conditioned to believe.

I start with my face, looking at the whole picture first...well, ok , stand back and focus. I see my eyes, they are not so bad. They are small, but the color of them is different and unique...a deep blue ring along the outside with green-blue and brown specks within, a hazel looking color. "Cat's Eyes"...that's what Cal saw. I look at my nose...it is a nice shaped nose. I have found something else I like about my face.

I have large lips, they are identically shaped like my Mother's were. She had beautiful lips I thought, so mine must be too. Big lips are in style now, models are collagen injecting their's to get lips like mine. I have found another thing about my face that isn't so bad. I take off my clothes, this will be a harder job.

I try to look at the whole picture...I find the scars, scars of my youth, scars from giving birth..then it dawns on me, these scars saved my life, saved the life of my unborn child. How can they be gross or ugly. They are battle wounds.

I find in looking at the whole picture of my body, that it isn't so bad after all. I am different, unique - not the perfect face or body, but unique is good. **I am me**...

If I am going to totally heal I have to look deep inside myself. I have to truly place the blame where it all goes, where it all started….my Father.

I had gotten angry at Rick and Mark and how they had treated me, but they treated me the same way my Father had . The same type of abuse I had come to expect in my life. I went out with men that would hurt me and shied away from men that might have truly cared. Ian had been the only one that had been good for me, and I had tried repeatedly to get him to leave me alone; but, he had the courage to stay and fight against my demons and all the walls I had built up around me…

I had to take the blame for my part in my and Chase's marriage and life falling apart so many times. I had suffocated him to the point in our marriage that he found the only route out that he knew…drinking. I had been a leech in our marriage and not a wife. I clung to him, in hopes of finding happiness through him and not in my own life. I made it impossible for him to have a sense of independence. I was just a kid, living in my own hell and expecting that Chase was going to rescue me and that I would live the fantasy with him and that true love always prevailed...but that is not true love. Love takes commitment and honesty...and a lot of hard work on both sides. If one or both are not willing to make the sacrifices, then no amount of love will ever make it work.

I had blamed Rick for all the things he did in our short marriage, but I found through all of this...I was to blame too. Yes, I was screwed up after Chase and I had split up, to messed up to begin another relationship so soon afterwards. But, I knew all along, deep down, that something was not right about this relationship. It had been wrong of Rick to use me...but it had equally been wrong to use him simply because I was too weak of a person to stand up on my own.

I also lay blame on myself with Mark. The signs were there before we were married. He had shown all the signs early on that he was trying to control me when he pouted over my spending time with friends. I had given into him and mistook control for love. I didn't deserve to be hit, true, but if I had realized the signs and acted on them before we got married, then there would have been no chance for me to be put in that relationship.

The signs for everything I had went through had been there prior to my making some of the decisions that I had made. The gut instincts were always there, I just ignored them.

I could never have stopped what my Father had done to me, and I certainly had no control over my Mother's overdoses. But, the one thing that could have stopped was what happened to my future. I had needed counseling, therapy...treatment. I needed to be whole again in order to embark on any relationship. I just didn't know that. I didn't know how to open up and tell anyone what was happening to me. In those days sexual abuse was never discussed.

Reliving it is what I had to do, letting the pain surface and learning to be whole again. Talking about it, getting angry about it... the only way to heal the person within. I had pushed the pain down within myself over and over again, making myself believe that I was past the damage and could move on, but without someone's help, that really is and impossible task. You cannot hide from it forever, at some point it will rear it's ugly head and cause the world to come crashing in...

Thank God for Ian, if he had not had the patience to sit there night after night and help me to deal with the pain, listen to me as I screamed and cried and hated my very own soul. I can't honestly say what would have happened to me...Thankfully, Ian also helped me to put my relationship with Hannah back together. We learned to rebuild our lives together, and since then she has married and given me four grandchildren to love and watch the innocence glow through thier eyes.

As the oldest daughter, Sierra recently celebrated 10 years of marriage and has added to her family with a son...taking my total of grandchildren up to six. With all my daughters and grandchildren, I can watch them grow and learn and develop their natural talents and zest for life. To be their own person, have their own personalities and their own sparkles in their eyes, free from any demons. Free from barriers, independant and out-going. Loving and emotionally stable, in life and in Love.

CHAPTER TWENTY FIVE

The final chapter of this book...**the help**.

The person within is your only ally . Reliving that past is what you have to do...letting out the pain and frustration. I am no longer afraid of my life now, thought the illnesses and traumas of life still exist.

I tell everyone that I know: "If you know of someone that has been sexually abused, physically, verbally or otherwise..get them the treatment they desperately need. Find a mental health agency, a doctor, a therapist...right now, **the sooner the better**." The chances for healing are so much stronger the earlier the intervention. No one can ever understand the pain of abuse. Especially when it is inflicted on a child. That child may appear happy and healthy....but they are not- I repeat..**they are not**.

Somewhere within them lies a volcano just waiting to erupt, sometimes buried so deeply within their subconcious that it takes a team of experts to get at the pain and in many cases, without treatment, that pain comes boiling to the surface and then it is much more than they can handle.

The victims of child abuse, any type of abuse, grow up and then start acting out in the strangest ways. I was lucky...I really was. I screwed up three marriages, I believed my existence was worthless...but I did live through it. I did get to the root of the pain and find a way to deal with it.

Now I am not saying I am completely healed, I have no idea if that is ever entirely possible. It is a daily struggle to maintain normalcy in my life.

So, no I don't think I ever will be completely healed, and will forever fight to remain independent. It is a daily struggle to stay strong and determined. But, each day makes me stronger and more resilient to what has happened in my past.

Self esteem and self worth are what are important for a person; destroy that and they are nothing more than the shell of what they can be in life, to easy for the victim to fall into the traps they set over and over again.

I could have easily become an alcoholic, it felt good to drink; I could have become someone different when I drank - it helped me to forget. I could have been the drug addict, the prostitute, the self- abuser. I could have also turned the abuse I suffered against my own children, and possibly could have abused them sexually or physically, and allow the patterns to emerge again and again…

But somewhere in my childhood…I gained courage; courage I didn't even realize I had, to endure the abuse I was going through.

Courage to know night after night what was going to happen to me and yet be able to function like a normal child during the day and hide the pain deep within myself.

I came out of the deep depression, with Ian by my side. I prevailed - stronger and more determined than ever to succeed at my life more than ever before. That's where this book comes from…the deepest region's of the pain.

Ian told me when I was up and around again, that I needed to write everything down on paper, make a journal or write it all in a diary. I have always been a writer, first of poetry and then of my own romance novels, always putting them in a drawer when I was finished writing each of them. Always believing I wasn't good enough as a writer to ever show my work to anyone but my family.

But I did take his advise and write, let it out of my heart, my soul.. and started this book..

Sometimes I find it hard to believe that with everything that we have been through, we somehow made it through and that we stood tall against some very hard forces in our lives...but we have endured.

There is one last thing that I would like to say in this book: Don't let a child be one more statistic...if you know the abuse has occured, even if you just suspect it, get help for that child **Now**. Talk to that child or young adult, find out if your fears are founded, and please get them the help that they so desperately deserve.

Now that I have come through this, I have come to realize that I will never look at the Homeless, the Prostitute, orthe Addict in quite the same way as I once did. The pain that they may have had to endure in thier childhood's, in thier lives...

Because **Nightmares do Echo**...

Printed in the United States
40169LVS00008B/2